ALEXANDRA WOOD

Plays include *Never Vera Blue* (Futures Theatre); *The Human Ear* (Paines Plough); *Ages* (Old Vic New Voices); a translation of Manfred Karge's *Man to Man* (Wales Millennium Centre); *Merit* (Plymouth Drum); *The Initiate* (Paines Plough, winner of a Scotsman Fringe First); *The Empty Quarter* (Hampstead); an adaptation of Jung Chang's *Wild Swans* (Young Vic/ART); *The Centre* (Islington Community Theatre); *Unbroken* (Gate); *The Lion's Mouth* (Rough Cuts/Royal Court); *The Eleventh Capital* (Royal Court) and the radio play *Twelve Years* (Radio 4).

Short plays include *Invitation Interrupted* (Donmar Warehouse); *The Driving Rage* and *Pope's Grotto* (Paines Plough); *My Name Is Tania Head* (part of *Decade*, Headlong).

Alexandra is a past winner of the George Devine Award and has been the Big Room Playwright-in-Residence at Paines Plough.

Alexandra Wood

THE TYLER SISTERS

NICK HERN BOOKS

London

www.nickhernbooks.co.uk

A Nick Hern Book

The Tyler Sisters first published in Great Britain in 2019 as a paperback original by Nick Hern Books Limited, The Glasshouse, 49a Goldhawk Road, London W12 8QP

The Tyler Sisters copyright © 2019 Alexandra Wood

Alexandra Wood has asserted her moral right to be identified as the author of this work

Cover image: istockphoto.com/ViewApart

Designed and typeset by Nick Hern Books, London
Printed in Great Britain by Mimeo Ltd, Huntingdon, Cambridgeshire PE29 6XX

A CIP catalogue record for this book is available from the British Library

ISBN 978 1 84842 927 7

The Tyler Sisters was first performed at Hampstead Theatre Downstairs, London, on 13 December 2019. The cast was as follows:

MADDY	Caroline Faber
KATRINA	Angela Griffin
GAIL	Bryony Hannah

Director	Abigail Graham
Designer	Naomi Kuyck-Cohen
Lighting	Joshua Gadsby
Sound	Jon McLeod
Movement	Angela Gasparetto

For Rachel

Characters

MADDY, *the eldest sister, twenty to sixty years old*
GAIL, *the middle sister, eighteen to fifty-eight years old*
KATRINA, *the youngest sister, sixteen to fifty-six years old*

The play is for three women to perform, the parts should not be divided up into 'younger' and 'older'.

A forward slash (/) indicates the point at which the next speaker begins.

This text went to press before the end of rehearsals and so may differ slightly from the play as performed.

1990

GAIL. You didn't even ask.

KATRINA. It's not your house.

GAIL. My room, / not yours

KATRINA. Not now.

GAIL. Not your house either, much mine as it is yours so you need to know your place.

KATRINA. Oh do I?

GAIL. Why d'you think you can just take what you want?

KATRINA. Because I can, I did.

And you weren't using it.

GAIL. I was though, my stuff was in there, I was using it to store my stuff.

KATRINA. Well I'm using it to sleep in, which trumps storing stuff, sorry.

GAIL. Where am I supposed to sleep all summer?

KATRINA. Wherever you want, you can sleep in my old room if you want, I don't mind.

GAIL. Don't mind? That's good of you, that's really / generous.

KATRINA. Does it really matter?

GAIL. It's my room, my place in the world.

KATRINA. Your place in the

A boxroom in your parents' house. Have a little ambition Gail.

GAIL. It isn't the boxroom, yours is the boxroom.

And I do have ambition, thank you. But for now, for now, that room is my place and you / can't just

KATRINA. You've got a room in Leeds.

GAIL. No I don't.

KATRINA. Where d'you stay then?

GAIL. Over the summer I don't, not till September.

KATRINA. Have mine till then, like I said.

GAIL. What about Maddy's? Why didn't you take that?

KATRINA. She's in it.

MADDY. I am in it, to be fair, I am actually in it.

KATRINA. Would've been a bit much to be all, vacate your room now Maddy, I'm taking over.

GAIL. But it's okay to do it to me?

KATRINA. Not the same, you weren't even here.

GAIL. We've established / that.

MADDY. I don't think it's the same, Gail, you weren't here.

And we didn't even know you were coming home this summer.

GAIL. Yeah, well, sorry, I am, I have, sorry to screw up your plans.

MADDY. What happened?

GAIL. I just love you all so much I couldn't stand to be away a moment longer.

MADDY. That's / nice.

KATRINA. Right.

GAIL. Just as well I did or you'd have Mum and Dad even more round your little finger. Didn't they say you should ask me at least?

KATRINA. Maybe, I don't know, I just did it, I didn't think it'd be such a big deal, but I should've remembered you like to overreact at the / slightest

GAIL. I'm not / overreacting

KATRINA. We thought you were in Leeds all summer, I was planning to come visit, but that's gone out the window / now I guess.

GAIL. Sorry to ruin your plans.

KATRINA. S'alright, going to Newquay instead.

GAIL. Who with?

KATRINA. Friends.

GAIL. Who?

KATRINA. You don't know them.

GAIL. Do Mum and Dad know them?

KATRINA. In what way?

GAIL. Do they know who they are?

KATRINA. Do any of us really know who we are Gail?

GAIL. Alright, alright, so how will you feel when I take my room back when you're in Newquay, how'd you think you're going to like that?

KATRINA. I won't like it at all.

GAIL. Yeah, that's gonna suck for you, isn't it.

KATRINA. I'd suggest you don't do that.

GAIL. Really?

KATRINA. Yeah, I'd suggest you leave my room well alone.

GAIL. Oh really? That's interesting that is, isn't that interesting Maddy?

MADDY. Um, I don't know if I'd say it was interesting.

GAIL. Yeah, no, I think that is. She can dish it out / but she

MADDY. People say lots of things are interesting but they say it in a way that I don't think they think it's interesting, so it's quite confusing.

KATRINA. Interesting, Maddy.

MADDY. Is it?

KATRINA. No.

MADDY. Oh. You see.

KATRINA. I had sixteen years in that poky little box, it's not fair, we should've swapped years ago.

GAIL. You got here last, not our fault.

KATRINA. Got here last? This isn't camp, I didn't get here late, I wasn't born.

GAIL. Camp? Don't say camp.

KATRINA. Back one minute and she's already telling me what to say.

GAIL. Don't say camp like that's a thing we do, a thing anyone we know does. I hate when people use American references they've blatantly just seen on TV.

KATRINA. I have been to camp, we both have, Brownie camp, so screw you.

GAIL. Are you going to apologise?

KATRINA. For what? Reminding you you were a Brownie?

GAIL. For stealing my room.

KATRINA. Are you still going on about that?

1991

GAIL. They left me in charge.

KATRINA. Maddy's in charge and she doesn't have a problem with it, do you?

MADDY. I

GAIL. They left both of us in charge.

KATRINA. Maddy doesn't have a problem with him.

GAIL. Well I do.

KATRINA. Is there anyone you don't have a problem with?

GAIL. Plenty of people.

KATRINA. Who?

GAIL. Maddy.

KATRINA. Yeah coz Maddy doesn't do anything / to upset you.

GAIL. I don't have a problem with you, it's him.

KATRINA. He's my boyfriend, are you going to tell me who I can go out with now?

GAIL. He's not your boyfriend.

KATRINA. Er, yes, he is.

GAIL. You might think he's your boyfriend / but he's

KATRINA. Fucking hell Gail, could you be more patronising?

GAIL. I just see it / like it is.

KATRINA. Coming from you. Coming from someone who can't even get a boyfriend at university, where there are literally thousands of horny guys left right and centre and you can't get one of them to / fuck you.

GAIL. It's not like that.

KATRINA. So you can get one to fuck you?

GAIL. He's not staying over while I'm in charge.

KATRINA. You're not in charge, and he is.

GAIL. Maddy, back me up here.

MADDY. He is her boyfriend.

KATRINA. Thank you.

GAIL. Whatever you want to call him, he's not staying over.

KATRINA. We call him Mo. Since that's his name and most people call people by their names.

GAIL. Mo?

KATRINA. You got a problem with that too now?

GAIL. That for the Mohawk is it?

KATRINA. Is that what offends you?

GAIL. No, no, the drugs offend me Katrina, the drugs, not his hair.

KATRINA. Weed? You're offended by weed? What kind of student are you?

GAIL. He does more than weed.

KATRINA. Expert are you?

GAIL. Do Mum and Dad let him stay?

KATRINA. They like him.

GAIL. Then they can't know him.

KATRINA. You don't know him.

GAIL. They let him stay?

KATRINA. He's stayed over before, yeah.

GAIL. While they were here?

KATRINA. What do you think he's going to do exactly?

GAIL. He was off his face.

KATRINA. So he was a bit drunk, big deal.

GAIL. It was more than that.

KATRINA. You're worse than Mum and Dad.

GAIL. You don't know how good you've got it.

KATRINA. Oh, you've had it tough have you?

GAIL. No, none of us have. So why are you hanging out with guys like him? What are you trying to prove?

KATRINA. Guys like him? Do you ever hear yourself?

GAIL. You know what I'm talking about.

KATRINA. Guys like him?

GAIL. You know what I mean.

KATRINA. What do you mean?

GAIL. He's a drug addict.

KATRINA. Because he smokes a bit of weed?

MADDY. Is he?

KATRINA. No.

GAIL. Come on.

KATRINA. He's not an addict.

GAIL. You might think I'm boring Katrina, but / you're the cliché

KATRINA. You are.

GAIL. You're using him just as much as he's using you.

KATRINA. How exactly?

GAIL. You think he makes you interesting.

KATRINA. That your oh-so-clever analysis is it?

GAIL. Nothing clever about it, / it's painfully obvious.

KATRINA. Well at least that's true.

Please.

GAIL. It is, it's embarrassing, when you look back at this
you're going to be embarrassed.

KATRINA. Well when you look back there'll be nothing,
nothing to remember.

MADDY. Stop it.

KATRINA. Your life, just this long blank, this long boring
blank of nothingness.

GAIL. Do what you want but you're not bringing him here.

MADDY. Please stop it.

GAIL. Let him use you if you want but I won't let him use this
house, no way.

KATRINA. Fine, I'll go to his. If that's what you want, I'll go
there.

MADDY. No.

KATRINA. You want to be in charge Gail, you explain that to
Mum and Dad.

1992

In the garden, sunbathing. There's quiet for a while.

KATRINA. What time is it?

> *Pause.*

> What's the time?

> MADDY *looks at her watch.*

MADDY. One-twenty.

KATRINA. When's lunch?

> I thought lunch was at one.

MADDY. Mum's making it.

KATRINA. Can you ask her where it is?

MADDY. I think she's still making it.

KATRINA. Okay, but can you ask her when it'll be ready then?

GAIL. Ask her yourself.

KATRINA (*shouts*). Mum. Mum.

> *Pause.*

> She can't hear me, could you just go in, you're halfway up anyway.

> MADDY *gets up and walks to the kitchen.*

> Thanks Mads.

> *Silence.*

> MADDY *returns.*

MADDY. She says we have to wait till Dad's back from the dump.

KATRINA. When's that gonna be?

MADDY. He should've been back at one.

KATRINA. He'll be talking to one of the men, he always gets involved in some long conversation about something one of them found and how people don't know the value of things and how it's a gold mine.

MADDY. It is a gold mine.

KATRINA. All he has to do is drive there, dump some stuff, come back, but no.

MADDY. You can find good stuff there.

KATRINA. Not when you're s'posed to be back by one so people can eat.

MADDY. Found those medals.

KATRINA. What medals?

MADDY. Military medals. Fifteen of them in that biscuit tin.

KATRINA. When?

GAIL. You don't remember?

KATRINA. Why would I remember a bunch of medals?

GAIL. She wore them for ages.

KATRINA. You wore a bunch of military medals?

MADDY *nods*.

Where?

MADDY *indicates her chest*.

Obviously there, where I mean, where did you go in these medals? Parades, memorial services, where?

MADDY. Everywhere. School.

KATRINA. School?

GAIL. How can you not remember this?

KATRINA. You wore military medals to school?

MADDY *nods*.

If that'd been me, they would've been confiscated in a minute.

MADDY. I said Granddad had died and I wanted to honour him.

KATRINA. But they weren't Granddad's.

MADDY. No, I found them.

GAIL. At the dump, which is why we're / talking about

KATRINA. Didn't people take the piss?

MADDY. Yeah but I just really loved them.

GAIL. D'you remember when Laura wore that black armband for like half a term?

KATRINA. Laura who?

GAIL. Maddy's year. Laura Laura

MADDY. Tait.

GAIL. Yeah, Tait, and she wore that black armband when her gran died, like she was Victorian or something, it was so fucking weird.

KATRINA. Was she the anorexic?

MADDY. No, that was Laura Peterson. Laura Tait was blonde.

KATRINA. Didn't know her. What's the time, I'm hungry.

MADDY looks at her watch.

MADDY. One-twenty-five.

KATRINA. Right, he's got till half-past then we're eating, I don't care.

1993

KATRINA. Wonder what it is. Drum roll.

GAIL unwraps a present.

GAIL. Love the paper.

MADDY. I made it.

GAIL. I know.

KATRINA. Likes to show us all up.

It's a woolly hat and scarf in purple and white.

GAIL. Amazing, look at these. And they're so soft, thank you.

MADDY. I heard it's cold there.

GAIL. Yeah, it can be.

MADDY. I did it in the university colours.

GAIL. They're perfect.

She tries them on.

How do I look?

MADDY *smiles.*

KATRINA. Purple isn't everyone's colour but

GAIL *hugs* MADDY.

GAIL. I'll miss you.

Pause.

KATRINA. I didn't make you anything.

GAIL. I didn't make you anything either.

KATRINA. You wouldn't want anything I'd made. And you won't need anything to remind you of me since I'll be visiting.

GAIL. Okay, let me settle in first.

KATRINA. Chill out, you've got till December.

GAIL. But can you just wait to see how I'm doing before you book anything?

KATRINA. Why?

MADDY. She might want the city to herself.

KATRINA. The whole of New York?

GAIL. I just

I haven't even got there yet, so can we just wait and see.

KATRINA. You said I could visit.

GAIL. Yeah, but I don't know what it's going to be like, it's a completely different continent and culture and I'm there to study, so

KATRINA. Please tell me you're not going to spend a year in New York studying.

GAIL. That's kind of exactly what I'm there to do.

KATRINA. Wasted on you.

GAIL. Maybe the summer's a better time to visit.

MADDY. I've heard it gets cold there.

GAIL. Exactly, it's cold in the winter, you don't like that. And by the summer I'll have the place figured out. Know all the best places to go.

KATRINA. I don't get why you don't want me there.

GAIL. I do but it's my

Thing

Alright? So

KATRINA. Alright.

GAIL. I just

I just want to be totally free to

Be whoever I want and

KATRINA. And I'd ruin that.

GAIL. No, but

KATRINA. It's cool. I just wanted to do some Christmas shopping, but you've made it into an existential drama as usual so I'll go to Oxford Street, / it's not a big deal.

GAIL. It's not a drama

MADDY. You want to be free.

GAIL. Exactly, I just want to, not start again but try new

No one knows me there so I can

KATRINA. No one knew you in Leeds.

GAIL. Yeah, but I was still a train ride away and everyone was, I don't know, I was eighteen so I didn't take the chance

KATRINA. I get it.

If I were you I'd want to be someone new too.

GAIL. Okay.

A long silence.

KATRINA. I get it.

GAIL. It's only a year.

1994

GAIL. Thought you might want to go somewhere else on your day off.

KATRINA. A: this is the best and basically only good bar round here. B: Tasha's working so we'll get loads of freebies, you're welcome by the way, and C: I wanted you to see Aaron.

GAIL. Who isn't here.

KATRINA. Yeah, well I didn't know he was going to be off sick, did I.

MADDY. I like it here.

KATRINA. So does Gail, she just likes to make a fuss.

GAIL. I do like it, I was just saying you spend a lot of time here so

KATRINA. Aaron says I could be manager by next year.

GAIL. If?

KATRINA. If nothing. If I continue to be as great as I am.

MADDY. That'd be cool. Having your own bar.

GAIL. She wouldn't own it.

KATRINA. I'd be the manager, what d'you mean if?

GAIL. He says you *could* be manager, which implies an if.

KATRINA. Does it?

GAIL. I wasn't trying to

You'd be a great, they'd be lucky to have you.

MADDY. A man asked me out.

KATRINA. What?

GAIL. Who? When?

KATRINA. It's always the quiet ones, isn't it.

MADDY. Rory. At work last week.

KATRINA. Last week and you didn't tell us?

GAIL. Probably never gave her a chance.

KATRINA. Who is he?

MADDY. Rory.

KATRINA. Yeah, okay, we've got that much. What's he do? How old is he? This is so cool. Or is it, are you interested?

MADDY *nods*.

Then it's very exciting.

MADDY. He's twenty-eight.

KATRINA. Okay, four years older, that's perfect.

GAIL. And he works with you?

MADDY. He looks after the school grounds.

KATRINA. Handy, that's good.

GAIL. How long have you known each other?

KATRINA. Why've you never mentioned him before?

GAIL. Probably because of this, this tsunami of / questions.

KATRINA. Is he fit?

MADDY *nods*.

GAIL. And how long have you known him?

MADDY. Since I started working there.

KATRINA. So like five years?

MADDY *nods*.

And has he flirted or, I mean have you only just decided you like each other or has it been five years of simmering sexual tension in the staffroom?

MADDY. I didn't really notice him at first. He was just Rory.

KATRINA. Okay, okay, that's cool, sometimes it creeps up on you. Like I didn't really notice Aaron at first, 'cause he's a nice guy, which isn't my type, but then he sort of won me over slowly when I saw there's more to him than nice, like he can be really authoritative when there's an arsehole in the bar, and I like that.

GAIL. So Rory.

KATRINA. Yeah, so what did he say when he asked you out, was it formal or

MADDY. We were in the staffroom at lunchtime, / eating

KATRINA. Romantic already.

MADDY. Eating our sandwiches. We sometimes share them, I give him half of mine and he gives me half of his, / so we

KATRINA. Mix it up, I like it.

MADDY. And he said, I think I'd like to ask you out Madeline.

KATRINA. Madeline?

MADDY. He calls me that.

GAIL. He thinks he'd like to, what, he's not sure?

MADDY. And I said, are you not sure?

GAIL. Good.

MADDY. And he said, let me rephrase that. I know I'd like to ask you out.

GAIL. Better.

MADDY. And then I said, go on then. If you know it's something you'd like to do. But then the bell went.

KATRINA. You're kidding?

MADDY. No. So we went back to work.

KATRINA. But

MADDY. But at the end of the day, we were in the staffroom again and he said, Madeline, will you go out with me?

KATRINA. And you said

MADDY. I said I'll think about it.

KATRINA. Seriously?

GAIL. Playing it cool, that's our sister.

KATRINA. So? Have you thought about it?

MADDY. Yes, and I don't think he's the one for me.

KATRINA. What?

MADDY. He's a bit quiet.

KATRINA. Are you

I can't tell if you're joking or

MADDY *smiles*.

GAIL. She's joking. She's in love.

MADDY *smiles*.

MADDY. I think I'm in love.

1995

Boxing Day. The film Beethoven *is on the TV.* MADDY *now wears a wedding ring.*

After a long time.

GAIL (*without taking her eyes off the TV*). We should probably play a board game or something.

No one responds.

MADDY *farts*.

They laugh.

1996

The day room of a care home. MADDY *is pregnant.*

KATRINA. You alright?

> MADDY *nods.*

> Maybe you shouldn't have come.

MADDY. I wanted to see her before he's born.

KATRINA. It isn't personal. I mean, everything she says is just

> She probably doesn't know who any of us are.

GAIL. She called us by our names.

KATRINA. But you can't take it personally, what she says,
that's all I'm saying. There's no filter.

GAIL. People say there's no filter like that's a bad thing, but
maybe it means we're just getting the undiluted truth.

KATRINA. No, I don't think that's

> What she said isn't what she'd mean, Maddy.

GAIL. How do we know?

KATRINA. Because it isn't.

> Because we know who she was, who she

> She never would've said that.

GAIL. She wouldn't have said it, no, but maybe she'd have
thought it.

KATRINA. No.

GAIL. So you know her thoughts now?

KATRINA. Why are you

GAIL. What?

KATRINA. It's hard enough.

GAIL (*to* MADDY). You're not the only one she's said stuff to,
Mum's had to put up with way worse and you're crying over
a few questions.

KATRINA. It's upsetting.

GAIL. Don't come if you can't handle it. Because it's not about you. It's about seeing Nan, while we can, so don't make it all about

And maybe she had a fucking point, I mean

Why the fuck are you pregnant?

Silence.

MADDY *leaves.*

KATRINA. Because she had sex with her husband, Gail.

That's how it works.

GAIL. It's a joke.

KATRINA. What is?

GAIL. Maddy.

KATRINA. What about her?

GAIL. Married, pregnant, I mean

Nan's right, what the fuck?

KATRINA. She's married and she's going to be a mum and you're

You're just

Pause.

Say bye to Nan for us.

KATRINA *leaves.*

1997

A party.

KATRINA. They're coming from through there. So if we stand right here we should get decent pickings.

The blond boy who looks fourteen, go to him, he wouldn't dream of pretending not to notice you. He's too innocent.

GAIL. I should've eaten before, I know what these things are like.

MADDY. I've got a cereal bar if you want.

KATRINA. Why didn't you say, I'm starving.

MADDY. Sorry, I didn't think.

KATRINA. Hand it over then.

GAIL. Please.

KATRINA. Now.

GAIL. Don't you want it Maddy?

MADDY. I'm alright.

MADDY *takes the cereal bar from her purse and* KATRINA *tucks in.*

KATRINA. Genius, thank you.

GAIL. Aren't you going to share?

KATRINA. No.

When do you think we can leave? Tasha's set me up with a guy from her gym.

GAIL. You always have somewhere else to be.

KATRINA *shrugs.*

This is Dad's night, why did you have to fit something else in as well?

KATRINA. I don't get many evenings off, I have to pack it in.

GAIL. You always pack it in.

KATRINA. Why don't you pack it in for once? Hey? Get it?

   Tough crowd.

MADDY. I can't stay too long either.

GAIL. Rory's fine.

MADDY. I know he is.

GAIL. We're hardly ever together, just us, can't we

KATRINA. Just us? There are loads of / people.

GAIL. But the three of us, / without

KATRINA. Do you know any of these people?

GAIL. A few.

KATRINA. I don't. Not a single one.

GAIL. You know us.

KATRINA. I mean his colleagues or his clients or whoever
   they are.

MADDY. That's his boss.

GAIL. How d'you know that?

KATRINA. He has a big B on his forehead.

GAIL. What?

KATRINA. I'm starving.

GAIL. How much champagne have you had?

KATRINA. Hard to tell isn't it, when they keep topping you up.

MADDY. They've topped it up a lot.

KATRINA. Thanks for keeping tabs Mads.

   Mads Tabs. You could run a business called Mads Tabs.

GAIL. You're going to be wasted before you even meet your
   date.

KATRINA. I'll have sobered up by then.

GAIL. How?

KATRINA. Nobody knows how it's done.

You could be this sober person people hire to keep tabs of how much they're drinking and when they've had enough, you can close their tab. It's brilliant.

GAIL. Great. Quality time with my sisters.

KATRINA. You're always going on about quality time, you need to get a life.

MADDY. Shall I get you some water?

GAIL. Sorry I want to spend time with you, what a terrible person.

KATRINA. No water necessary. Some food would be nice, but I think it might be an unrealistic dream.

MADDY. I'm sorry if I don't see you enough.

GAIL. It's not you Maddy.

KATRINA. Are all dreams unrealistic?

MADDY. I know it's not the same now.

KATRINA. They should be, dreams should be unrealistic, otherwise they're realistic, which is the opposite of a dream, so

MADDY. Mum and Dad spend a lot of time with Connor.

GAIL. He's their grandson, it'd be weird if they didn't want to.

MADDY. But maybe it seems like he's taking over.

GAIL. I love Connor, okay?

I mean Dad loves him so much he's basically giving up work to spend more time with him but

MADDY. No, that's not / why.

GAIL. I'm joking, of course he's not. I mean, a little bit, but not really.

KATRINA. It's good he's giving up work, lucky bastard.

MADDY. It's not because of Connor.

GAIL. I was joking, Maddy.

MADDY. He didn't want to retire.

GAIL. He seems pretty happy about it.

KATRINA. What do you dream about Gail?

MADDY. They offered him early retirement but he didn't have much choice about it.

GAIL. He told me he couldn't wait.

KATRINA. Do you think there's a kitchen behind that door or is it just a dream?

GAIL. Why did he tell me that if he was forced into it?

KATRINA. Gail?

GAIL. Shut up Katrina.

KATRINA. Shhhh.

GAIL. Go drink some water will you?

KATRINA. I don't need water, I've had a cereal bar.

GAIL. Why didn't he tell me he was forced to leave?

MADDY. He's looking at the good side. More time with Mum, Connor, us.

GAIL. But it wasn't his choice. Why's he even here, celebrating with them? Why are we here?

KATRINA. Good question, maybe the food's coming from somewhere else, is there another door?

GAIL. Thanks for all your decades of work, and now let's celebrate by pretending we all get on one last time. Cheers.

KATRINA. Cheers.

GAIL. It's just a massive fucking charade.

MADDY. You're not angry at him are you?

KATRINA. That'd get this party started, charades!

GAIL. No, Maddy, I mean he lied to my face, but

MADDY. Please don't be angry at him.

GAIL. I'm not, okay, don't worry.

KATRINA. Three words girls, three words and it's a

She mimes the sign for film.

Alright?

GAIL. Film, got it.

KATRINA. You're always good at things like this. Okay, so it's a film and it's

She holds up three fingers.

GAIL. Three.

MADDY. He was probably a bit embarrassed.

GAIL. Got it.

Three words.

KATRINA. Actually, no, crap, it's not three words, it's three

She mimes syllables.

Yeah? Syllables. Cool. So first syllable.

GAIL. He's not embarrassed around you though, is he.

KATRINA. Okay girls, focus.

She mimes putting bait on a fishing hook and casting the line.

GAIL. Fishing.

KATRINA. Yeah, but what am I putting on the hook?

GAIL. A worm?

KATRINA. Yeah, yeah, but what is that?

GAIL. Bait?

KATRINA. Yes, fucking genius. Okay, Bait. Remember that. Now second syllable.

MADDY. Should you be allowed to talk?

KATRINA. Should you?

MADDY. Yes, that's part of the game.

KATRINA. Okay, so second syllable.

She thinks about how to mime 'Ho'.

Fuck. This is hard, I forgot how hard this was. I can't do this shit on an empty stomach.

MADDY. It's because he respects you, he cares what you think, it's a compliment.

GAIL. He doesn't trust me enough to be honest.

KATRINA. Maybe we should mime food, if we mimed eating d'you think we'd still be hungry?

1998

GAIL*'s flat. They're eating dinner.*

KATRINA. Thought Jonathan might've taken you out.

GAIL. Yeah, he did offer.

KATRINA. But you said you'd rather stay in?

GAIL. He is taking me out, just not tonight.

KATRINA. Because?

GAIL. Because I'm seeing you guys.

KATRINA. We wouldn't have minded.

GAIL. I wanted to see you.

KATRINA. Okay.

GAIL. Why'd you always have to make me feel like that's sad somehow?

KATRINA. Just if it were me, I'd've chosen the date with my new handsome boyfriend.

GAIL. Yeah well we're different.

KATRINA. That's very true.

MADDY. When are we going to meet him?

GAIL. We're just seeing how things go.

MADDY. Mum and Dad can't stop going on about it. Keep telling all their friends he's a CEO.

GAIL. It's only been three months.

MADDY. But you like him.

GAIL. Of course I like him.

MADDY. So that's good isn't it?

GAIL. Of course it's good.

KATRINA. So why'd you seem kind of pissed off?

GAIL. I'm not.

KATRINA. It's 'cause it's her birthday and she's always miserable about it.

GAIL. I'm not miserable for God's sake.

KATRINA. No, you're over the moon.

GAIL. I am. I'm doing cartwheels, alright, I'm jumping for joy on top of the world and walking on air and cloud nine okay?

How's the food?

KATRINA. Sorry, just to be clear, you're walking on air, but you're also on a cloud?

GAIL. Yes.

MADDY. And you're jumping, but at the same time you're doing cartwheels?

GAIL. Yes.

KATRINA. I'd love to see that.

GAIL. You are seeing it, that's what I am, right now.

KATRINA. Yeah, but I'd love to actually see it.

GAIL. Well I'm eating so

KATRINA. So you're eating while you're jumping but also doing cartwheels?

GAIL. Very clever.

KATRINA. We have got to see that.

GAIL. Now?

KATRINA. I think so, yeah. Maddy?

MADDY. Yeah, I think so.

GAIL. Fine.

She gets up.

KATRINA. So you're eating.

GAIL *eats some food.*

MADDY. And jumping.

GAIL *jumps.*

KATRINA. While continuing to eat.

GAIL. I'll be sick.

KATRINA. And

MADDY. And doing cartwheels.

KATRINA. You must be so happy, only a very happy person would do all this at once.

GAIL *stops.*

Don't stop.

GAIL. I can't even do cartwheels at the best of times.

KATRINA. But this is better than the best so you'll probably just magically be able to do them.

GAIL *jumps a bit and does a very ropy cartwheel.*

KATRINA *and* MADDY *cheer.*

Not bad.

GAIL. It was pathetic.

KATRINA. Yeah, but how long since you've done one of them?

GAIL. I feel sick.

KATRINA. That'll be the joy. It does that.

GAIL. I can do a better one, let me try again, wait a sec.

KATRINA. Getting in to it now.

GAIL *does another cartwheel, which is slightly better, if only for the extra enthusiasm. Her sisters cheer.*

Well, we stand corrected, you're obviously as happy as you say. We've seen it with our own eyes.

GAIL *sits down again.*

GAIL. I like him, I do.

KATRINA. But he's got a small dick, hasn't he.

GAIL. But I guess I just sort of think

Is this what I've waited for?

1999

A country pub.

GAIL. What d'you think?

MADDY. Whiskey isn't really my thing.

GAIL. Jonathan said we had to try it at least.

MADDY. I'm sure it's nice, if you like whiskey, but I don't really.

GAIL. I've got more in to it since being with him, but it's not my favourite. What d'you think?

KATRINA *nods.*

What brands do you serve in the bar?

Pause.

They distil it here, it's won loads of awards. I mean I don't know which ones. I don't know what awards they have for alcohol, but it's won loads of them.

MADDY. Mum said you haven't been going in.

KATRINA. No, because I quit.

Pause.

GAIL. Probably time for a change anyway.

KATRINA. A change.

Has there ever been a less adequate word?

Silence.

MADDY. It was nice getting the train.

I like trains.

Just looking out the window, don't have to worry about traffic or

KATRINA. I can't get in a car so

MADDY. That's totally

GAIL. Just give yourself time Katrina.

Pause.

KATRINA. Should've come away just the two of you.

GAIL. Why would we do that?

MADDY. We need you.

KATRINA. Well I'm not me.

MADDY. You are.

KATRINA. No Maddy, I'm not.

MADDY. You will be.

KATRINA *shakes her head.*

You're still here.

KATRINA. Why? Tasha's not, so why am I? What's the point?

Silence.

We were the same. We did everything the same. Slept with some of the same guys, not at the same time, but we did think about it. Worked the same shifts, wore the same clothes, went to the same parties, she was more than my sister, because we don't do the stuff Tash and I did, we shared more than I've shared with anyone, and in a second she's gone. No more.

What am I supposed to do on my own?

MADDY. You're not on your own.

KATRINA. I am though.

A long silence.

2000

In the observation tower at a paintballing venue.

MADDY. Do you think she minds?

GAIL. I bet she hasn't even noticed we're not doing it.

MADDY. I don't want to be a killjoy.

KATRINA. We're here aren't we.

MADDY. But we're not really entering the spirit of it.

GAIL. The spirit of it?

They're shooting each other with paint to celebrate her getting married.

MADDY. It's bonding. And we're not bonding, we're just watching.

GAIL. We're going to the meal later. We can bond then.

MADDY. I was surprised she invited us.

KATRINA. Auntie Pam probably told her she had to.

MADDY. But it's nice, so I feel bad.

KATRINA. Then go and do it Maddy, go run about and get shot, but don't sit here telling us you feel bad, what's that do?

Pause.

MADDY. My foot really does still hurt to run on.

GAIL. We'll be there for the meal.

MADDY. What is it again?

GAIL. A Mexican place.

MADDY. Great, coriander over everything.

GAIL. Okay, could we try not to be so fucking miserable for a minute? Do you think we could manage that?

Silence.

They watch below. They see Louise get shot and they wince, then laugh.

MADDY. We shouldn't laugh.

GAIL. But there is something funny about watching Louise get shot.

MADDY. It looks painful.

GAIL. I'm telling you now, if I ever get married and you're organising my hen, I don't want to do this.

KATRINA. Fine by me.

MADDY. Do you think that's on the cards?

GAIL. A wedding?

MADDY. Yeah.

GAIL. No, I mean, I don't

Maybe.

KATRINA. God help us.

GAIL. Don't say that.

KATRINA. You know we're fond of Jonathan but you know what he's like.

GAIL. But he's a good guy.

KATRINA. Who am I to say? I've never had a serious relationship.

GAIL. Say it anyway.

Pause.

KATRINA. Auntie Pam was being all positive that I'm at uni, going on about how I'm going to do great things with my life.

MADDY. Just trying to be nice.

KATRINA. I know but I just wanted to say, you don't get it, I'd swap seats with Tasha in an instant if I could.

2001

GAIL. Is it worth keeping these for the boys?

MADDY. Your roller skates? You can't give those away.

GAIL. I'd forgotten I even had them.

She looks them over.

Probably a bit scuffed up to pass on.

MADDY. Well-loved but maybe a bit.

You could still use them.

GAIL *tries them on.*

KATRINA. Where are we supposed to store all this stuff now?

GAIL. Get rid of it if you don't want it.

KATRINA. But I don't know what I'll want.

Maybe I'll want this in a few years' time.

MADDY. Really?

KATRINA. Maybe. I don't know, that's the point, I don't know how much of this stuff I'm going to need.

MADDY. Just go through it and see.

KATRINA. Okay for you.

GAIL. They're a bit snug, but

She attempts to stand up.

MADDY. Steady.

GAIL. I'm alright. Check me out, I'm alright.

MADDY. Careful.

GAIL *roller-skates around the room a bit.*

GAIL. It's all coming back to me now.

She skates around humming Celine Dion's 'It's All Coming Back to Me Now'.

MADDY (*to* KATRINA). Do you want me to help?

KATRINA. How would you know what I'll need if I don't?

MADDY. It's not really about what you need, is it, you don't need any of this stuff.

KATRINA. I do.

MADDY. Okay.

KATRINA. You're gonna have an attic and a garage so what do you care? You can keep everything.

MADDY. Not really.

GAIL. Hey guys, watch me turn.

She turns and MADDY *applauds.*

MADDY. Very good.

KATRINA. This stuff actually means something to me. It's my life.

MADDY. No one's saying you have to get rid of it all.

KATRINA. But I do though don't I, 'cause where will it go? My tiny room in the new house?

MADDY. It's not tiny.

KATRINA. There isn't room for this.

MADDY. Well you could move out.

You're free to find somewhere bigger Katrina.

KATRINA. How am I supposed to pay for that?

GAIL *starts to sing the chorus of 'It's All Coming Back to Me Now'.*

GAIL. Sing with me.

She's roller-skating around the room. She keeps singing.

KATRINA. It's alright for Mum and Dad to support you but God forbid I should live at home while I'm studying.

GAIL throws her arms around KATRINA as she continues to sing the refrain.

Get off.

More singing from GAIL.

What's wrong with you?

As GAIL finishes the chorus, she moves away from KATRINA and does a spin.

(*To MADDY.*) They're only moving to help you, they don't want to go, you do know that, don't you.

MADDY. It was their idea.

KATRINA. You could've said no.

MADDY. Would you rather we had to move to the other end of the country?

KATRINA. What's wrong with the other end of the country?

MADDY. You're here that's what's wrong with it. We don't know anyone there.

GAIL starts the second verse of the song.

GAIL. It's so weird how you can remember lyrics, I haven't even thought about this in years and it's just right there.

She continues to sing and MADDY joins in, finishing the verse and starting the chorus again.

KATRINA. Are we doing this or not?

They stop for a moment.

GAIL. I don't know Katrina, it depends. If you want me like this, and you need me like that, it was dead long ago, but it's all / coming

KATRINA. They are actually leaving, you get that, right? This is it. So you can sing Celine Dion like it's really funny but it's not.

2002

The London Marathon.

GAIL. This is a bit better I guess.

MADDY. What time should he be here?

GAIL. Around ten-thirty if it's going to plan.

MADDY. Okay.

GAIL. He's in a bright-yellow top.

KATRINA. No costume?

GAIL. No, he's taking it pretty seriously.

KATRINA. I only came to see him dressed as a chicken.

GAIL. I never said he'd be dressing up.

He's going for a time. He's lost a stone.

MADDY. Like he needed to.

GAIL. I think he looks a bit sick to be honest.

MADDY. There are quite a lot of bright-yellow tops.

KATRINA. What time?

GAIL. Half-ten.

KATRINA. No, for the whole thing.

GAIL. Oh, three and a half hours.

KATRINA. Is that good?

GAIL. For a first marathon, yeah.

KATRINA. So this is his new thing?

GAIL. I hope not.

KATRINA. It'll be something new next month, don't worry.

MADDY. Is that him?

GAIL. Where?

MADDY. There, near the Postman Pat.

GAIL. No.

MADDY. There are so many people.

GAIL. I thought Rory and the boys were coming.

MADDY. Fergal didn't sleep last night.

KATRINA. Neither did I, don't see me complaining.

MADDY. Okay, but he's three so

GAIL. Why didn't you sleep?

KATRINA. Had a date.

GAIL. All night?

KATRINA. Yes Gail, all night.

GAIL. Is that

No. He wants a picture as well, so get out your cameras.

MADDY. I haven't got my / camera.

KATRINA. It was actually a fourth date.

MADDY. The guy from work?

KATRINA *nods*.

GAIL. Is that a good idea? You've only just started there.

KATRINA. You just worry about spotting your stick insect Gail.

MADDY. What's his name?

KATRINA. Can't remember.

MADDY. Are you

KATRINA. Of course I know his name. Fuck's sake. Nishok.

GAIL. Nishok?

KATRINA. Yeah.

MADDY. There's four yellow tops coming up.

GAIL. So he's

KATRINA. What?

GAIL. Where's he from?

KATRINA. Southall.

GAIL. I'm just asking.

MADDY. Do you think we could sit down for a bit?

KATRINA. Yes, please could we do that.

GAIL. After we've seen Jonathan.

KATRINA. What time is it?

GAIL. He'll be here any minute, if we haven't missed him.

MADDY. I'm just feeling a bit faint.

GAIL. Sit down then.

KATRINA. There's a bench over there.

GAIL. Can you wait two minutes then we'll get a coffee?

KATRINA. It was a long night.

GAIL. You said, but you've made the effort to get here, don't you want to see him at least?

KATRINA. Honestly?

GAIL. He's running twenty-six miles, the least we can do is wave once.

MADDY. I'm just going to sit here for a

She lowers herself to the ground and sits there trying to stop the world spinning.

GAIL *keeps her eye on the runners.*

KATRINA. Tell me when he's here.

She sits next to MADDY.

2003

Fergal's bedroom. Connor's sixth birthday party is in full swing downstairs.

GAIL. I love his chair, look at it, it's so small.

MADDY. He never sits in it, he never sits anywhere.

She collapses onto the floor and holds up a bottle of wine and three glasses.

KATRINA. You said we weren't allowed.

MADDY. The kids can't see.

She pours the wine and hands it out.

GAIL. Happy birthday Connor.

They drink.

Is Rory alright down there?

MADDY *shrugs*.

KATRINA. They're exhausting. I'm exhausted.

MADDY. You've been here an hour.

KATRINA. Is that all?

She lies down on the floor.

Cool, he's got those glow-in-the-dark stars.

MADDY. You gave them to him.

KATRINA. Did I?

MADDY. For Christmas.

KATRINA. That was nice of me.

MADDY. Rory put them up so they're in the same position as the real stars.

KATRINA. What d'you mean?

MADDY. So if you could actually see the stars from here, they'd be in that position.

KATRINA. How's he know?

MADDY. No idea.

KATRINA. That's kind of cool.

MADDY. When I'm lying here waiting for Fergal to sleep,
I look up and imagine I'm on a beach somewhere staring up
at the stars. I say, tonight Matthew, I'll be in Costa Rica and
there I am.

GAIL. God we loved that, didn't we. Tonight Matthew I'll be
Diana Ross.

KATRINA. Can you shut the curtains.

MADDY. Don't, I'll fall asleep.

KATRINA. But I want to see them glow.

GAIL *shuts the curtains and the room gets darker. The stars
sort of glow.*

MADDY *lies down on the floor next to* KATRINA.

MADDY. This is dangerous.

KATRINA. It's tricky because I want to lie down but I also
want to drink and you can't do both at the same time.

GAIL. It's a cruel life.

They stare up at the glowing stars.

MADDY. Jonathan's good with the boys.

He's the only person I've ever seen match their energy.

GAIL. Yeah, he's good with kids.

MADDY. That's a good thing, isn't it?

GAIL. Sure, if we ever have them, it'll be great.

MADDY. He wants them doesn't he?

GAIL. In theory. Not yet. Always not yet.

Pause.

KATRINA. They're not that bright, are they. I should've got
more expensive ones, sorry.

MADDY. I know it's annoying to hear, but you've still got
loads of time.

GAIL. That's what he says.

MADDY. I know it's annoying to hear.

GAIL. I just don't see what we're waiting for.

MADDY. Does he want to get married?

GAIL. In theory. Everything in theory.

Pause.

KATRINA *sits up to drink. She lies back down.*

KATRINA. Comfy carpet.

MADDY. It's wool.

KATRINA. Yeah, it's nice. Not too scratchy.

Pause.

Least you're with someone.

GAIL. I guess.

KATRINA. You're closer than me.

Quiet.

They lie, watching the glowing stars and listening to the sounds of a six-year-old's birthday party.

2004

A student art show.

GAIL. Yours are the best by a mile.

MADDY. No.

GAIL. Really.

KATRINA. I don't get how you can just do it, how you can just draw like that without trying.

MADDY. I do try.

KATRINA. Yeah, no, I know, but you're a natural, you've always been able to draw, that's what I mean, you've either got it or you don't.

MADDY. I have a lot to learn.

KATRINA. Doesn't look like it.

MADDY. I do.

KATRINA. Well if I could draw like you, I'd be very happy.

GAIL. Has Rory been yet?

MADDY. He's bringing the boys on Thursday.

GAIL. What's he think of them though, he must've seen them.

MADDY. Not really, I did most of them in class.

KATRINA. He'll love them, why wouldn't he.

MADDY. Some of Fergal's drawings are better than mine.

GAIL. He's five, Maddy.

MADDY. They are though.

GAIL. Okay, but this is about you, not Fergal, and these are the best in the room.

MADDY. Have you seen Dan's?

GAIL. Those?

MADDY. They're amazing, aren't they.

GAIL. They're well framed.

MADDY. But look at the detail, it's incredible.

GAIL. Not my taste.

MADDY. He's already sold four and no one ever sells any at these shows.

GAIL. How much for?

MADDY. I don't know.

GAIL. Yeah, well there you go then.

KATRINA. I could buy some of yours for the hotel.

MADDY. What?

KATRINA. Yeah, that's a brilliant idea. I could buy your drawings for the bedrooms.

MADDY. Why?

KATRINA. Because they're good, idiot.

MADDY. Not that good.

KATRINA. Course they are.

GAIL. You're in charge of decor now?

KATRINA. I'm the manager, I'm in charge of everything.

GAIL. Yeah, but you're not a designer.

KATRINA. It's a few pictures on the wall Gail. And you never know what might come from it either. A guest likes it, asks where it's from, we could sell it for you too.

GAIL. Art dealer too.

MADDY. You don't have to do that.

KATRINA. I want to. How much?

MADDY. Seriously, Katrina.

KATRINA. I am serious.

GAIL. Why don't you check first, before promising something you / can't

KATRINA. Check with who? Myself?

How much Maddy?

MADDY. I have no idea.

KATRINA. Well you should think about it.

MADDY. They aren't ready for that.

KATRINA. Look ready to me.

GAIL. Maybe it's something to think about for the future.

KATRINA. I've been thinking the hotel needs a more personal touch and this is perfect. Original artwork by a local artist.

MADDY. I'm not an artist.

KATRINA. What are you then?

MADDY. I'm just

I just do it to relax.

KATRINA. How come you're showing it here then?

GAIL. It's a student showcase Katrina, not the Royal Academy.

MADDY. It's part of the class.

KATRINA. Yeah, because art's meant to be enjoyed, what's the point if no one ever sees it?

MADDY. Just because.

KATRINA. You could do with the money couldn't you?

MADDY. Is that why you're

KATRINA. That's not why I'm saying it, but you could, couldn't you?

GAIL. She doesn't want to sell.

MADDY. I could introduce you to Dan.

KATRINA. I don't want his work, I want yours.

MADDY. I'm just

I'm still learning.

KATRINA. Yeah, so's Picasso, so's that bloke with the sharks in the formaldehyde, he's definitely still learning, so?

GAIL. Such a critic.

KATRINA. Fuck off Gail.

MADDY. Don't be annoyed with me. Please.

KATRINA. I'm not annoyed with you, it's just frustrating, that's all.

GAIL. What's frustrating?

KATRINA. You're really talented and you don't see it, and it's just

GAIL. She's doing better than us, isn't she?

KATRINA. Yeah, of course you are, but that's not hard, I mean

Pause.

Doesn't matter, it was just an idea.

2005

KATRINA. You could put posters up at his work, letting everyone know what he's done. Or access his water supply somehow and poison it.

MADDY. We need serious suggestions.

KATRINA. These are serious. You could slash his tyres. Give all his clothes to a charity shop, I mean all his clothes. Do you still have his keys?

GAIL *shakes her head.*

Okay, no problem, we could break in.

MADDY. I said serious.

KATRINA. I am, it's not that hard, and I bet you, in fact I guarantee you if we were caught and the police came and we told them what he's done, they'd say go for it, do what you came to do. So we'd get in and just destroy everything in there, slash his mattress and sofa and curtains and spray-paint all over the walls and smash his kitchen up starting with his bottles of rare and wanky whiskey and flood the bathroom, and pour engine oil all over the carpets and trash his TV and records and throw his fucking guitars out the window and burn all his know-it-all guides to doing every fucking thing under the sun except how to be a decent person, which he clearly never heard of, the one fucking thing he never heard of, and then tear up his lawn and his plants and have a massive bonfire and invite everyone in the neighbourhood so they know they're living next to a sociopath and find his address book or hack into his email account and write to everyone he knows to let them know what a bad fucking person he is and maybe we could pay for an ad on the local radio station to spread the word further, and maybe organise a rally in the local park, we could do banners, Maddy you can make those, and just chant and walk the streets and let the people know Jonathan Bruce is a coward and a fake, a fake person.

These are just ideas.

MADDY. Has he asked how you are?

GAIL *shakes her head.*

I don't understand how someone can be like that. I really

KATRINA. I also thought, we could kidnap him and find a well somewhere remote and just drop him in it. With any luck he'd break something in the fall, but wouldn't die immediately, so it'd be a long and painful death.

MADDY. Let's not talk about

KATRINA. I've got a whole list. They might not be original ideas, but if it gets the job done, what's it / matter.

GAIL *gets up suddenly and goes to the bathroom to throw up.* MADDY *and* KATRINA *hear.*

She comes back and slumps down.

Pause.

Mum said the sickness is mostly just the day after.

GAIL. It's not that bad.

Pause.

KATRINA. Another thought I had, and this is a bit more expensive, but I heard of someone doing this once, is hiring one of those annoying bands, Mariachi, I don't know how you say it, but you hire a band and they play outside his bedroom window at 3 a.m. every night for a couple of hours so he can't sleep.

Could be any music he finds annoying. Again, just brainstorming.

GAIL. He's not worth it.

KATRINA. Beheadings, decapitations, is that the same thing? I'm available for all acts of revenge.

GAIL. I don't want revenge.

KATRINA. Of course you fucking do, he's the worst kind of person there is, he's not even a kind, that suggests there are other people like him, when he's his own category of shit.

GAIL. Relationships end all the time.

KATRINA. Yeah but not when

Come on.

GAIL. We should've broken up years ago, I don't know why we didn't.

KATRINA. Because he kept saying he wanted the same thing as you. He kept lying.

GAIL. He's not lying now.

KATRINA. Oh no, he tells the truth when it suits him, when it's the easiest option.

GAIL. I don't want him sitting at my bedside cleaning up my sick if he'd rather be somewhere else.

KATRINA. I know but come on!

GAIL. What?

KATRINA. You're fine with him just walking away?

GAIL. I've got bigger things to worry about.

MADDY. He's not important.

GAIL. And if I get better

KATRINA. When.

GAIL. If.

KATRINA. Don't say that, you need to believe / you're going to

GAIL. If I get better, I don't want to waste even more time on an average relationship, and if he had stuck around and if he had sat by my side and if he had cleaned up my sick I probably would've felt like we should just see it through, so I'm grateful he didn't, because if I get better, I'm free.

KATRINA. You will.

GAIL. And if I don't, I don't want him representing me, I wouldn't want him speaking about me, receiving condolences for me, being in any way associated with me, so thank God, that's what I think, thank God he's a coward and he left. Thank God.

Silence.

MADDY *reaches for* GAIL's *hand.*

2006

11 p.m. on Christmas Day. MADDY *and* KATRINA *play on the boys' new Wii. They're boxing: punching the air aggressively, taking it very seriously.*

GAIL *enters with a hot chocolate, sits and watches them, laughing at the ridiculous movements.*

KATRINA *wins.*

MADDY. There you go, you won. Can we stop now?

KATRINA. God yes.

2007

A café by the sea in Valencia.

MADDY. The boys would like this.

KATRINA. Sangria?

MADDY. Ha ha. The beach.

KATRINA. Are you a sangria expert now?

GAIL. Not really. Trying to be healthy. Not drinking that much.

KATRINA. Right.

GAIL. Okay, not this weekend, but generally.

Bring them Maddy, one of the holidays. They could do Spanish lessons.

KATRINA. Fergal would be fluent in a few days. It's crazy how absorbent that kid is.

MADDY. He does take things in.

KATRINA. When I took them to the Tower of London, when you guys were at that wedding, we were just walking about, nothing intense, didn't want it to be like a school trip or anything but afterwards he literally recited all the info from all the boards, which kings and queens had been there and the dates of everything, it was scary.

MADDY. He only has to read things once.

KATRINA. He's scary smart. Poor Connor.

MADDY. Connor doesn't mind, it's actually sweet, he's really proud of him.

Fergal was in this national maths tournament at school and he got to the final and Connor told everyone about it. He isn't jealous.

KATRINA. Connor's my favourite.

MADDY. Don't say that.

KATRINA. Okay, but he is.

GAIL. You could send them both for a week in the summer or something. You and Rory wouldn't have to come.

MADDY. Don't offer unless you mean it.

GAIL. I do.

KATRINA. I thought this was just a year thing.

GAIL. Maybe not.

KATRINA. You're staying?

GAIL. For now.

MADDY. And you can keep working at the school?

GAIL. They're always needing people.

KATRINA. Well it's not a bad place to visit I guess.

GAIL. And it's not too far.

MADDY. You seem happy.

GAIL. I am.

MADDY. More chilled.

KATRINA. Laid-back Spanish life.

GAIL. Suits me I guess.

MADDY. And have you met any nice people?

KATRINA. Jesus Maddy you sound like a mum.

MADDY. I am a mum.

KATRINA. Not Gail's. Bloody hell. Is there any talent, is what she wants to know.

GAIL *smiles*.

I fucking knew it, soon as I saw you, soon as I

But I know what you're like, I thought, I'll let her say, I won't probe, I'll be patient.

GAIL. Very restrained of you.

KATRINA. Yeah, it was. So?

GAIL. There is someone.

KATRINA. About fucking time.

GAIL. She's the school principal.

KATRINA. I fucking knew it.

GAIL. You knew she'd be a principal?

KATRINA. I knew she'd be a she, I knew it.

GAIL. Really?

KATRINA. Yeah, I just knew.

GAIL. How?

KATRINA. Sisters know stuff like that.

GAIL. Did you?

MADDY. I didn't, I mean, no.

KATRINA. And she's your boss? Are you kidding me, this is too good, she's your boss?

GAIL. Not technically my boss, / she

KATRINA. She employs you?

GAIL. But it's not like she's telling me what to do every day / or

KATRINA. And the hard time you gave me about Nishok.

GAIL. That was different.

KATRINA. No, I'm sorry, can we just take a moment here to apologise to Katrina, can we just take time out to say, I'm sorry Katrina, for criticising and judging when you fell for your boss, I'm aware I look like a hypocrite now.

GAIL. Okay, yeah, maybe I was a bit judgemental.

KATRINA. Wow, this is

This is amazing, are you hearing this Maddy?

MADDY. What's her name?

GAIL. Valeria.

MADDY. And she's from here?

GAIL. She's not from here, but she's Spanish, yeah.

MADDY. But she speaks English?

GAIL. She runs an English-language school.

MADDY. Right.

KATRINA. Anything else?

MADDY. I just

Have you told Mum and Dad?

GAIL. Not yet.

MADDY. But you're going to?

GAIL. Of course I'm going to.

KATRINA. They won't have a problem with it, I mean she must
be better than Jonathan, not that that says much, but after
him, I mean anyone you / bring home

GAIL. I wanted to tell you in person Maddy.

MADDY. It's cool.

How long have you been

GAIL. Six months.

KATRINA. You must've met her on your first day here, since
she's your boss and all.

GAIL. She's not my

But yeah, she's one of the first people I met, we didn't have
a proper conversation for a few months, but then on one of
the socials, we were both, not chaperoning, but we were the
two members of staff, and we were chatting and just, it felt
so easy and simple and uncomplicated.

KATRINA. Did you know she was gay?

GAIL. She's bisexual, but I didn't know that, I felt something
between us but at first I wondered if it was me as an English
person thinking that it was something more than it was, just
because we were getting on and I felt comfortable, I thought
maybe all Spanish people are just this easy to connect with
and it probably would've taken me months to do something
about it, although I still maintain I would've said something
eventually

KATRINA. But I mean the stakes were higher for you
obviously, because she's your boss.

GAIL. She's not my boss, but yeah, I guess I was a bit nervous about that, so luckily she made a move first.

KATRINA. Which was risky for her, as your boss, sexual harassment and all that.

GAIL. She asked if I wanted to go for a drink and I didn't really know what that meant, I thought it could be a group thing, / but

MADDY. But it wasn't.

GAIL. No. No, it wasn't, so yeah, I guess that was our first date.

MADDY. So you're living here now?

GAIL. Well, yeah.

MADDY. But not just for a year out, like properly living here.

GAIL. I hadn't really thought about it like that / but

MADDY. Because that's quite a big thing.

GAIL. Is it?

KATRINA. It's not any different Maddy, / it's

MADDY. But she might never come back.

KATRINA. It's / only Spain.

GAIL. We've only been going out six months, let's not

And who knows, maybe we'll live in England in the future.

MADDY. So it's serious?

GAIL. Is that okay?

MADDY. Of course it is, I just want to know.

GAIL. Then yes, Maddy, it's serious.

2008

A sauna.

GAIL. It's too hot.

KATRINA. That's the entire point.

GAIL. I might pass out.

KATRINA. Thought you'd be used to heat by now.

GAIL. Not ninety degrees.

KATRINA. I love it.

MADDY. We've got pedicures in fifteen minutes anyway.

KATRINA. Did you have to book so many things?

MADDY. Just wanted to make the most of the time.

KATRINA. So shhhh.

Let's enjoy it for a minute before we have to race to the next thing.

MADDY. We are enjoying it.

KATRINA. In silence.

MADDY. What's the point of that, it's basically our only time to catch up properly Gail's whole visit.

KATRINA. Okay, not true, but

MADDY. Pretty much.

GAIL. Just for a few minutes Mad.

They lie in silence for a minute.

MADDY. Feels weird just lying here.

KATRINA. Embrace it.

MADDY. It's hard.

KATRINA. Yeah, well, try.

Silence.

MADDY. Do you think Mum's looking older Gail?

KATRINA. Fuck's sake.

MADDY. I see her all the time so it's hard for me to tell.

GAIL. A bit maybe, she looks alright.

MADDY. Izzy said it the other day, she hadn't seen Mum for ages and she said she didn't recognise her.

KATRINA. Charming.

MADDY. Not in a good way.

GAIL. How long?

MADDY. I don't know, ten years maybe.

KATRINA. Ten years? Bloody hell, course she looks different, so do we.

MADDY. She doesn't.

KATRINA. Who?

MADDY. Izzy.

KATRINA. Good for her.

MADDY. She doesn't though, she looks twenty.

KATRINA. This'll help you look younger Mads, but it only works if you're quiet.

MADDY. I'm not a child.

KATRINA. Shhh.

Silence for a short while.

MADDY. What type of pedicure are you going to have?

GAIL. I didn't know there were different types.

MADDY. Yeah.

GAIL. Just the normal one I guess.

MADDY. Katrina?

Pause.

GAIL. I think she's trying to be quiet.

MADDY. So you don't think Mum looks older?

GAIL. Maybe a bit, I don't know.

MADDY. They are getting older.

GAIL. Don't write them off yet.

MADDY. But they are, they will.

GAIL. Alright Mads, what's up with you?

MADDY. Nothing.

KATRINA. She feels old 'cause she's got a kid in secondary school.

MADDY. No, just because Gail doesn't see them as much, she might notice a change.

GAIL. Alright Maddy, we get that I don't live here, we get I don't see them as much as you.

MADDY. That's not what / I'm

GAIL. I haven't noticed a change, okay?

Pause.

MADDY. I'm done.

She gets up and leaves.

GAIL. What's up with her?

KATRINA *shrugs.*

They endure the heat in silence.

2009

KATRINA *is pregnant.*

KATRINA. D'you remember when you were pregnant with Connor and we went to visit Nan in that home?

MADDY. Yeah.

GAIL. Vaguely.

Did she ever meet him?

MADDY *shakes her head.*

MADDY. I know Mum wished he was a girl.

GAIL. What, Nan reincarnated?

MADDY. Not really just

He was born a couple of days later and

Might've been nice.

GAIL. I mean they couldn't be more different.

MADDY. Well, no, they do look pretty different.

GAIL. Not even that, Connor's lovely and Nan was

KATRINA. Nan.

GAIL. To put it nicely.

MADDY. Just at the time it might've been nice. For Mum.

GAIL. You should count yourself lucky, you would've had to use Nan's name if he was a girl.

MADDY. That's true. Not that I got much say over it anyway.

KATRINA. Didn't you like Connor?

MADDY. I do now 'cause it's him but

Not really.

KATRINA. You better believe I'm not naming my baby something I don't like.

MADDY. It was a family name, Rory really wanted it.

What made you think of that?

KATRINA. What?

MADDY. Visiting Nan.

KATRINA. Was just thinking about what she said and how
I might feel if it was me and how my baby won't know Nan

GAIL. Lucky.

MADDY. Neither did my boys.

KATRINA. No, I know, and that's just the way it is

GAIL. What did she say?

MADDY. Who, Nan?

GAIL. Yeah.

MADDY. Just

She didn't even know what she was saying.

GAIL. But you remember it?

MADDY. Yeah, but it's not fair because it wasn't really her.

GAIL. What was it?

MADDY. She just asked

You don't remember?

GAIL. No.

MADDY *nods*.

KATRINA. She asked her why she was pregnant.

GAIL. What, like, how?

MADDY. No, why.

GAIL. Okay. I mean, that doesn't really

MADDY. You asked me too.

GAIL. Why you were pregnant?

MADDY. Yeah.

GAIL. No I didn't.

MADDY. Yeah, you did.

GAIL. Well I have no idea what I meant.

I mean I don't remember it but

I hated seeing her in there, it was fucking

No one deserves that.

Sorry. Sorry if it hurt you or

MADDY *shrugs*.

Did it?

MADDY. You knew it did. You might've forgotten now, but you did know.

GAIL. Well I have forgotten.

MADDY. I believe you.

KATRINA. I don't think it's such a bad question.

MADDY. What?

KATRINA. Not a question someone else should ask you, but I was thinking about it.

MADDY. Bit late for that.

KATRINA. No, I know, I'm not saying anything, I'm just

Make you think all sorts of shit, these hormones.

2010

A campsite.

MADDY. I know it's not your thing.

KATRINA. I can rough it now and again.

MADDY. But with Walter as well, it's not ideal.

KATRINA. It's your birthday Mads, not mine.

GAIL. Where've Mum and Dad gone?

MADDY. Took the boys for a walk.

KATRINA. Who needs dogs when you've got Connor and Fergal.

GAIL. I don't think there's enough food for tonight.

MADDY. There's leftovers from last night too.

GAIL. Leftovers for your fortieth, bloody hell Maddy, we can do better than that can't we?

KATRINA. Are they still alright to eat?

MADDY. They'll / be fine.

GAIL. Where are Mum's car keys, I'll go to that place we went yesterday, pick up some extra steaks, maybe some fish.

MADDY. The boys won't eat that.

GAIL. For the grown-ups.

MADDY. I really don't think it's necessary.

GAIL. I'll pay Maddy, it's fine.

Pause.

MADDY. We don't want waste.

GAIL. It'll get eaten.

MADDY. It's not about money it's about waste, there's nowhere to store it and no one's going hungry, are they, I think we'll all just about manage to survive.

GAIL. Fine, it's your birthday, not mine. If some bangers on the BBQ's all you want, that's cool.

MADDY. It is all I want. And to spend time with my family. Which I'm doing. That's enough for me.

GAIL. A lover of the simple things.

MADDY. What's wrong with that?

GAIL. Nothing at all, very noble.

MADDY. / Noble?

KATRINA. Simplicity's the ultimate sophistication. Read that in an ad, but I think it's an actual quote by one of the Greeks.

The sound of the baby crying in the tent.

MADDY. I'll get him.

KATRINA. Just see if he settles first, he needs more sleep.

The baby continues to cry throughout the rest of the scene.

MADDY. There is actually extra food anyway, I planned for nine.

GAIL. Lucky Valeria couldn't make it then.

MADDY. Yeah, guess so.

GAIL. What is there to drink?

MADDY. Wine, beer, soft drinks.

GAIL. Champagne?

MADDY. We're camping Gail, this isn't The Ritz.

GAIL. You've got to have a toast on your birthday.

MADDY. Do I?

GAIL. Yes. That shop might have some, am I allowed to get that at least?

MADDY (*to* KATRINA). Are you sure he's okay?

KATRINA. Just give it a minute.

MADDY. I hate hearing babies cry.

KATRINA. Really? 'Cause I love it.

Just give it a minute.

GAIL. Where are Mum's keys?

MADDY. I wouldn't know.

Why can't you just sit down and be with us?

GAIL. Yeah, it's really peaceful.

KATRINA. Fine, I'll get him.

She gets up and goes to the tent. The crying dies down.

MADDY. Just sit down for a minute.

GAIL *sits down.*

You never sit down.

GAIL. What am I doing right now?

MADDY. Okay, because I asked.

GAIL. A birthday treat.

MADDY *smiles.*

Pause.

MADDY. I'm sorry she couldn't make it.

GAIL. Yeah, me too.

Silence.

Work's

There always seems to be something.

They sit for a while.

Is everything alright with

She gestures towards KATRINA *in the tent.*

MADDY *shrugs.*

GAIL *nods.*

They sit for a while.

2011

KATRINA *and* MADDY *watch Connor play rugby.*

MADDY. I know she's annoyed.

KATRINA. She'll get over it.

MADDY. But she is.

KATRINA. It's not as if you've never visited Mads, it's fine.

MADDY. She thinks it's because I don't like Valeria.

KATRINA. You don't.

MADDY. I don't know her.

KATRINA. 'Cause she never makes the effort to come here.

MADDY. Go Connor! Run, run, go on! Ahh…

KATRINA. Nearly.

MADDY. Well done Connor, keep it up!

He hates me cheering, I shouldn't do it.

KATRINA (*cheers*). Go Connor!

MADDY. We shouldn't do it, he gets funny.

KATRINA. You know I'd get the flight.

MADDY. You don't have to do that.

KATRINA. If you want to come and you're worried Gail will never forgive you, you know I'd get it.

MADDY. I know.

KATRINA. I won't say it again, but I'm putting it out there.

MADDY. Thank you. I know you would.

They watch Connor.

KATRINA. Is he still going?

MADDY. He says he is.

KATRINA. He has to.

MADDY. He knows that.

Get him Connor, go on!

KATRINA. But he doesn't have access to your account now.

MADDY. Oh God, that looks painful. Some of the boys he plays against now are bigger than Rory.

KATRINA. I know you don't want to talk about it.

MADDY. It's not like we lost the house.

KATRINA. You could've.

Still could if he's not getting help.

MADDY. He is.

And I'm aware now, aren't I, so

KATRINA. They're good liars.

MADDY. He's not a liar.

KATRINA. Addicts are good liars.

MADDY. He's not an

Can we drop it?

KATRINA. Connor can't hear.

MADDY. Please.

KATRINA. Okay.

Pause.

MADDY. He's a good man.

KATRINA. Yeah.

MADDY. A good dad.

KATRINA. Not that great if your kids lose their home, but

MADDY. Better than Eric.

KATRINA. He never wanted

It's different.

I was never under any illusion he'd be there for Walter.

MADDY. But you had him anyway?

KATRINA. Would you rather I hadn't?

MADDY. Don't be ridiculous.

Pause.

KATRINA. I've always liked Rory but when it comes to it I'm looking out for you, and the boys, but you, Mads, okay.

2012

Stonehenge car park.

GAIL. It's good to do tourist stuff now and again.

KATRINA. Don't think I've ever even been.

GAIL. Mum said we came one summer, when I was four.

KATRINA. So I was two, Walter's age, not surprised I don't remember that.

GAIL. He might remember this.

KATRINA. Doubt it.

GAIL. Doesn't change though, does it. We're looking at the exact same thing now as we were then.

KATRINA. Gift shop's probably improved.

MADDY. Do you think Val will be long in there?

GAIL. They've been here four and a half thousand years, hard to get your head round.

KATRINA. Don't get how they managed it.

GAIL. Four and a half thousand years.

KATRINA. I can just about get my head around a hundred but anything beyond that

GAIL *sings a section from 'Stonehenge' by Ylvis. She makes the words 'technology' and 'today' rhyme with 'high'.*

What?

GAIL. That song by Ylvis on YouTube, haven't you seen it?

KATRINA. About Stonehenge?

MADDY. The traffic on the A303 can be hell.

GAIL *sings another few lines*.

KATRINA. What?

GAIL. It's brilliant, it's this completely over-the-top song about this guy who has everything but he's plagued by the meaning of Stonehenge.

MADDY. Gail.

GAIL. Ask the boys, I bet they've seen it.

GAIL *laughs*.

KATRINA. What?

GAIL. No, it's just in the video, he's got this perfect wife and kids and earns loads of money but all he ever thinks about is Stonehenge. Just watch it, I can't explain it, but it's funny.

MADDY. How much time can you spend in a gift shop?

GAIL. It's fine Maddy, relax.

KATRINA. Do I need the loo? Can I be bothered with the queue, that's the question.

GAIL. Just go, there's nothing worse than needing the loo and being stuck in traffic.

MADDY. Well, I mean, there probably are worse things, / but

GAIL. Just go, now you've thought about it you'll need to go so you might as well just go. Val usually gets sidetracked reading anyway so you've got time.

KATRINA. You're right.

KATRINA *exits*.

MADDY. I told Mum we'd be back by seven.

GAIL. Okay.

MADDY. So how sidetracked does she get?

GAIL. There's loads of time Maddy.

MADDY. Yeah but she does kind of run on Spanish time, doesn't she.

I know it's just a cultural thing, but Mum's getting more and more particular about times and it's better for everyone if you just get there when she asks.

GAIL. And we will.

MADDY. Honestly, it's been getting a lot worse. Punctuality, it's all she'll talk about. I'm just saying it so it's been said.

GAIL (*exiting*). I'll see how she's doing.

2013

They make sandwiches. KATRINA *butters the bread,* GAIL *does the filling,* MADDY *cuts them and arranges them on platters. They do this in silence.*

After a while, KATRINA *breaks down. She does her best to recover quickly and blows her nose.*

MADDY *opens a large packet of crisps and tips them into the bowl.*

GAIL. They'll go stale if you open them now.

MADDY *takes some cling film and puts it over the bowl.*

They go back to making sandwiches.

2014

KATRINA *and* GAIL *share a bottle of wine.*

KATRINA. I don't know why he does it, it's exhausting.

GAIL. I swear he didn't draw breath, we were walking to preschool and he just narrated the whole thing, 'and now we're crossing the road, this is a fun crossing, sometimes Neil's here, he likes to wear yellow' and then we pass this guy, and he's a big

KATRINA. Shit, he's done this / before.

GAIL. And Walter's like, 'and some people in this town have an obesity epicdemic'.

KATRINA *laughs.*

And the guy totally hears, as does everyone else, but Walter just looks up at him and asks his name. And the guy's obviously completely confused by this, he just says Joe, in this really small kind of unexpected voice, for such a big guy, and then Walter goes ahead and introduces him to the non-existent camera, he says 'This is Joe, say hi to the camera Joe' and so Joe just kind of waves / and it's this

The doorbell goes.

KATRINA. God I love him.

She gets up to answer the door.

I mean it's going to get him in trouble one day, but it's pretty cute right now.

(*Offstage.*) Oh hey, didn't know you were dropping by.

MADDY (*offstage*). Didn't you?

KATRINA (*offstage*). No.

(*Offstage.*) It's Mads.

GAIL. Hey. We've just opened a bottle, d'you want some?

MADDY *and* KATRINA *enter.*

MADDY. Having a relaxed evening are you?

GAIL. Have you heard the reality-TV-narration thing Walter does?

MADDY. He does it all the time.

GAIL. It's so cute though, today we passed this fat bloke

She gets up to kiss MADDY.

Are you alright?

MADDY. Why wouldn't I be?

GAIL. Okay.

D'you want a drink?

MADDY. I'm driving.

GAIL. A small one?

MADDY shakes her head.

Pause.

KATRINA. Okay, well, shall we sit down at least?

She sits, GAIL *follows.*

Gail was just in the middle of the walk to school, so this Joe bloke's waving to an imaginary camera?

GAIL. Yeah, that was all really, it was just pretty surreal.

I'm not used to Walter's ways yet, I'm sure he's been doing it a while.

MADDY. We've all got our little ways.

GAIL. True. Nice to get to know him better, silver lining, he's quite the character.

Pause.

KATRINA. Are you going to sit down Maddy or you just going to stand there awkwardly?

MADDY. You didn't think I'd drop by?

KATRINA. No, sorry, had we said?

MADDY. After today, you didn't think I might pop over?

KATRINA. After

MADDY. Today.

KATRINA. Today.

MADDY. With Connor.

KATRINA. Okay. That's between me and Connor.

MADDY. My son.

KATRINA. It was at work, it was within a professional environment.

MADDY. Your nephew.

KATRINA. I gave him a chance. More than one. I gave him warnings.

GAIL. What's wrong with him?

MADDY. Oh nothing, his aunt fired him, but obviously that's not a big thing to her, big shot over here, hires and fires all day, what's Connor matter.

KATRINA. Oh come on.

MADDY. Well he doesn't, does he, not really.

KATRINA. He was late, Maddy.

MADDY. He's eighteen.

KATRINA. What's that got to do with it?

MADDY. Everything.

KATRINA. He was late every day this week, even after I warned him. What was I supposed to do?

MADDY. Give him a chance.

KATRINA. Hopefully he'll learn from it.

MADDY. What's he supposed to learn? / That his aunt doesn't believe in him, that his

KATRINA. Not to be late, I would've thought that was pretty clear.

MADDY. That his aunt's embarrassed by him, that he's not good enough?

KATRINA. I was embarrassed and I told him that.

Linda came to me, and it was awkward for her, but she said Connor's been late every day and it's not fair to the others if I don't discipline him.

MADDY. So discipline him, you don't have to fire him.

KATRINA. We treated him the same as any employee.

Look I'm sorry Mads, I didn't like having to do it, but he was taking the piss.

MADDY. It was his first job.

The number of times you messed up at his age.

KATRINA. I'm not denying that.

MADDY. And here you are preaching about what's fair and he's embarrassed you, couldn't you have just let it go? He needed that job, Katrina, you know that more than anyone. We needed it.

Pause.

KATRINA. He'll get another one.

MADDY. Oh you'll write a glowing reference will you?

KATRINA. I'll help him Maddy.

MADDY. Like you did today? He doesn't need that kind of help, thanks.

She goes to leave.

KATRINA. Don't go.

GAIL. You need a drink.

MADDY. No I need a son in work.

GAIL. Okay, but failing that

She offers her glass. MADDY *takes it and downs the wine.*

Oh right, so that's

MADDY. He has no confidence as it is, having Fergal for a brother's hardly easy, suicide's the biggest killer of young men, / and it's getting

KATRINA. Okay, he's not, let's just

MADDY. What if it was Walter?

What if I'd fired your son, would you be sitting there sipping your wine thanking me for teaching him a valuable life lesson?

KATRINA. Probably not.

MADDY. So don't tell me to calm down.

KATRINA. I didn't.

MADDY. He's my boy and you, you said, I was what mattered to you Katrina, you said that, well he's me, he's part of me, so why would you throw him away?

Pause.

Enjoy the wine.

She exits.

A long pause.

KATRINA. Fuck.

Pause.

Fuck.

She gets up.

Watch Walter?

GAIL *nods.*

KATRINA *exits and we hear the sound of the front door shutting.*

2015

The film Bridesmaids *plays but no one watches it.* GAIL *and* KATRINA *are on their phones,* MADDY *sketches.*

This goes on for a while.

MADDY (*without looking up from her sketchpad*). Shall I turn it off?

GAIL. Why?

MADDY. No one's watching.

KATRINA. I'm listening.

> MADDY *continues to sketch and they continue to play on their phones.*

2016

Sunbathing, the South of France.

MADDY. It does feel weird though.

KATRINA. He would've wanted her to be happy.

MADDY. But I think she's

> *Pause.*

KATRINA. What?

MADDY. I don't want to say it because

> It was Dad, so

KATRINA. But?

MADDY. I think she's happier than she was with

> I guess I've never really seen her like this.
>
> This happy.
>
> Is it just me?

KATRINA. No, she is, she does seem to be

She's different.

Pause.

It's not disloyal to say it, we're just seeing what we're seeing and just because he was our dad and we loved him doesn't mean he was perfect for Mum.

MADDY. But that makes me

Doesn't that make you

Silence.

GAIL. It's so fucking hot.

KATRINA. How did you do eight years in Spain?

GAIL. I wasn't lying about sunbathing all day.

She sits up.

This place is pretty amazing, no wonder she's in to him.

MADDY. Mum's hardly a / gold-digger.

GAIL. I'm kidding.

But it's romantic, isn't it.

Hard not to be swept up in it.

KATRINA. And why not?

GAIL. Dad never had any of this to sweep her off her feet.

MADDY. Not about that, she's not that shallow.

GAIL. Exactly, but if she'd met Henri twenty, thirty years ago this probably wouldn't have appealed in the same way it does now.

KATRINA. Really?

A villa in the South of France, a good-looking gentleman to wine and dine you, that wouldn't appeal?

Pause.

You need to stop saying his name like that.

GAIL. Henri.

KATRINA. It winds Mum up.

GAIL. I don't do it to his face.

Pause.

Henri.

KATRINA. Just lose the accent.

GAIL. It's no fun that way.

Pause.

He's definitely a homophobe.

MADDY. Why?

GAIL. He is.

KATRINA. He's fine with Somesh.

GAIL. What's that got to do with it?

KATRINA. Just saying, he's been nothing but charming to us.

GAIL. So he's not overtly racist, great. Doesn't mean he's not a homophobe.

KATRINA. Does he even know you're gay?

GAIL. Oh yeah, soon as I arrived it was 'shame you don't have a lady friend at the moment', which was just totally creepy. Shame for who? Him? And at the restaurant last night we had that really camp waiter, and he kind of nudged me and said don't know how he manages to carry trays of food with wrists that limp.

KATRINA. We were all pretty drunk, to be fair.

GAIL. That's not cool Katrina.

MADDY. Did you say anything?

GAIL. No, I didn't, 'cause Mum was there.

MADDY. Should've said something if it bothered you.

GAIL. So it's my fault he's homophobic?

MADDY. What?

GAIL. He's a seventy-year-old man, I shouldn't have to tell him that's obnoxious.

MADDY. He's a different generation.

GAIL. So he gets a free pass to be a total dick?

Pause.

KATRINA. He makes Mum happy.

GAIL. I'm only here for her, believe me.

KATRINA. I mean, the gorgeous villa helps but

GAIL. I don't need any of this.

KATRINA. But it is nice though.

GAIL. So?

Surprised she's fallen for someone as smug as him.

MADDY. Least he's generous.

GAIL. Dad was generous. Sold his bloody house to get you one so

MADDY. Wow. Okay.

Silence.

GAIL. Too hot. Sit in the shade for a bit.

GAIL *exits.*

2017

They make name cards for a table setting, MADDY *does most of the work.*

MADDY. Who?

GAIL. So I was waiting for Walter in the playground, and there were all these mums and dads, mostly mums, and Jonathan, Jonathan is standing there on his phone.

KATRINA. Jonathan? As in

GAIL. Yes.

KATRINA. Fuck.

GAIL. Yeah.

MADDY. As in your Jonathan?

GAIL. Not my Jonathan but yeah.

KATRINA. Has he got a kid at St Mary's?

GAIL. Two.

KATRINA. Two?

GAIL. Ten-year-old boy, five-year-old girl. Course he's got one of each.

KATRINA. Oh my God that makes sense.

MADDY. Did you speak to him?

GAIL. Course I bloody did.

KATRINA. Because I saw this kid in the playground, and when I saw him I was instantly reminded of Jonathan, it was the weirdest thing because obviously I never really think about him, but he just came into my head, and that must've been his son, he's the spitting image.

MADDY. Have you got any more twine?

KATRINA *passes her a ball of twine.*

GAIL. Yeah, so I went up to him and he couldn't believe it.

KATRINA. How long's it been?

GAIL. Twelve years.

KATRINA. That long?

MADDY. I can't believe that.

GAIL. Obviously a lot's happened. He was completely, he obviously had no idea what to say.

KATRINA. I mean where do you begin?

GAIL. He just said how are you and I said, alive. 'Cause he wouldn't have even known if I'd died, would he, we just cut contact, so how would he know.

KATRINA. I can't believe I've probably walked past him in the playground or been at a carol concert or something when he's been there.

GAIL. His wife normally collects them, he said.

KATRINA. So how much did you get in to, did you get to Valeria or

GAIL. No. Walter came up and he asked if he was my son and Walter obviously put him right but we couldn't really get in to much.

MADDY. Keep making as you talk guys, we've got loads to do.

GAIL. And then his kids came over too so it was kind of hard to

He was so relieved to see them, they looked kind of confused.

KATRINA. So you didn't say anything, you didn't

GAIL. Not really.

KATRINA. I mean you went out for like

GAIL. Seven years.

KATRINA. So his son's ten? So he moved on pretty quick.

GAIL. Doesn't surprise me. So as we were leaving I said, oh, give me your number, let's get a coffee, catch up properly, and you could tell he was really confused and was all like, oh, it's the same number I've always had and I said, yeah I think I deleted it, can I get it again.

MADDY. You're not gonna call him?

GAIL. No.

I just wanted to see his face.

KATRINA. I bet I'll see him loads now.

MADDY. Focus guys.

GAIL. Mine are shit Mads, you're better at this.

MADDY. I can't do all of them.

GAIL. I bet you could if you tried.

MADDY. I've got the table decorations to do as well.

KATRINA. Somesh said can you get him the list of what you
need by next week, his mum's bringing it from India.

MADDY. I already sent it.

KATRINA. Oh sorry, I didn't realise, he just said it this
morning so

MADDY. I sent it this afternoon.

KATRINA. Perfect.

GAIL. I've felt really weird the whole afternoon.

KATRINA. It is weird when stuff like that happens.

GAIL. He's done everything he said he wanted to do, get
married, had kids, but with me it was always not yet.

MADDY. Maybe he just sensed something wasn't right between
you, I mean you wouldn't have been happy with him if
you'd done that whole thing.

GAIL. I might've been.

MADDY. Oh come on.

GAIL. I might've been.

MADDY. After what he did?

GAIL. No, not after what he did, but if we'd just got married
and had kids and I'd never got sick and he'd never acted the
way he did I probably would've been happy enough.

MADDY. But he's not a good person. Someone who does that,
you would've found out one way or another eventually.

GAIL. Maybe, maybe not.

I mean what've I got now that's so good?

Twelve years, what've I done?

2018

MADDY *and* GAIL *are in the women's toilet at a bar.*

MADDY. I can't

It just makes my blood boil, I'm sorry, I can't

GAIL. It's alright, Maddy.

MADDY. No, it's not, it's really, how dare he, how dare he?
Everything I do, every sacrifice I make to keep our heads
above water and he just blows it all in an empty gesture, he just

GAIL. Breathe.

MADDY. He's just got no idea, no idea, what he puts me
through, he says he does, he says he's sorry, he says we're
everything to him but that's obviously not true and I've only
got myself to blame, that's the worst of it, I can't / even

GAIL. Can we just breathe, Maddy, can we just / do that?

MADDY. What's the point? I cut back on everything I possibly
can, I count pennies, I do that, I count pennies, do you know
how that feels, at forty-eight years old, like a child at a sweet
shop, I count pennies but he spends two hundred pounds on
champagne in a second and doesn't think twice. Two hundred

GAIL. We'll work it out, okay.

MADDY. Two hundred pounds? Who does he think he is? Mr
Big Man, Mr I-Can-Keep-Up-With-You, well you can't Rory
you can't, these people have better jobs than you, these
people earn more and know how to save and plan and look
after their finances in a way you never will, you / can't

GAIL. Forget the champagne, alright, we'll sort that out
between us.

MADDY. Even if he'd let you, which he won't, because he's
a proud bastard and he'll savour that moment, when all he
should feel is shame, but he won't feel that, he has no idea
what it's cost me and I'm not talking about money, what it's
cost me, I'm talking about me, my being, and do I get
moments I can forget, do I get moments I can act like a
normal, generous person and buy a drink for my family like

it's no big deal, do I get those little moments of light where things are normal? No because he takes them when we can't afford them, he's taken so many of those moments I'll never get another one again

KATRINA *enters.*

KATRINA. Just wondering if you were alright?

GAIL *shakes her head.*

MADDY. Same as always, nothing new.

KATRINA. We'll split the bill Maddy, I know he got carried away, but we wouldn't expect you to pay that.

MADDY. No of course you wouldn't, 'cause I never pick up the tab, do I, I can never treat my sisters and that's what makes it even sadder, isn't it, he acts the big man and doesn't even realise he's not fooling anyone. I can't go out there, I can't look at him I can't stand to look

GAIL. We can stay in here for a bit, tell them I've got diarrhoea.

MADDY. I need to get out of here.

KATRINA. Don't let it ruin it, Mads.

MADDY. He's ruined it.

KATRINA. We're all here, we'll pay for the champagne one way or another, so we might as well enjoy it. How often do we get a night out together?

MADDY. Never and why's that? Because we can't, his mess means we can't, and if we do he manages to make things even worse so what's the point, really, what's the point?

KATRINA. For two hundred pounds it probably tastes pretty good.

MADDY. He doesn't even like champagne.

KATRINA. More for us then.

Pause.

Come on.

Don't let him get to you.

MADDY. When do I just

Pause.

When's it too much?

KATRINA. You'll know.

2019

Karaoke booth. They're singing Backstreet Boys' 'I Want It That Way'.

KATRINA *knows it the best,* MADDY *and* GAIL *join in but are less confident, while* KATRINA *even knows some of the dance moves.*

As it ends…

KATRINA. Tasha loved that.

2020

Evening, in the car, KATRINA *drives.*

MADDY. I think you could've mentioned.

GAIL. What's to mention?

MADDY. That she could be your daughter. I mean she must be Connor's age, is she?

GAIL. She's older than that.

MADDY. How old is she?

GAIL. So you don't approve, what a surprise.

KATRINA. She seemed really nice.

GAIL. She is.

KATRINA. I liked her Gail.

MADDY. Look of course she's nice.

GAIL. So what's the issue?

MADDY. When you said she was one of your students I thought you meant one of the mature ones.

GAIL. She's not a child Maddy, I'm not dating a child.

MADDY. Okay, but how old is she, twenty-five?

KATRINA. I really liked her.

MADDY. Why wouldn't you, she's like an excitable puppy.

GAIL. What's wrong with that?

KATRINA. I think I fancied her a bit.

MADDY. She is gorgeous.

KATRINA. And her skin, bloody hell, it was all I could do to stop myself stroking her face.

MADDY. I didn't understand every word she said but she seemed very sweet.

GAIL. We communicate perfectly.

MADDY. Good.

GAIL. It's never felt so easy.

MADDY. Good, I'm really pleased for you Gail, I am. You deserve it.

GAIL. Men go out with girls twenty years younger all the time and no one bats an eyelid.

MADDY. Twenty years?

GAIL. I'm not forcing her into a relationship, what do you think, I'm bribing her to go out with me?

MADDY. Come on.

GAIL. She likes me, I like her, what's the problem?

KATRINA. There isn't one.

MADDY. I don't want you getting hurt.

KATRINA. Maddy

MADDY. I don't.

GAIL. Why would I get hurt?

MADDY. Because you're

Okay first off, isn't this breaking the teacher–student code?

GAIL. She's left the college, and I never even taught her personally.

MADDY. Alright, but she's here for, for how long? She came here to learn English, okay, well she seems to have done that pretty well.

GAIL. You just said you couldn't understand her.

MADDY. You know what I mean, and so what's the plan?

GAIL. There isn't one.

MADDY. Great, okay.

Pause.

KATRINA. Can you imagine what Henri's going to think of her?

GAIL. Oh God.

KATRINA. How happy he'll be you're bringing a lovely lady to his lair.

GAIL. Oh God.

MADDY. Don't call it a lair, what's that make Mum?

KATRINA. His prey. Or no, what is it when you've already caught it?

GAIL. His spoils?

KATRINA. His booty. His booty, oh God.

MADDY. He's not that bad.

GAIL. I wanted you to meet her.

Because you never got a chance to know Valeria, not properly, but I did love her.

KATRINA. We know you did.

GAIL. Obviously the distance meant you never really got to know her the way I wanted and I'm not saying that's why we broke up, it was more complicated than that, obviously, but after Dad, and how it was at the funeral, she just wasn't

But I'm here now and Paola's here, we can go for dinners and hang out and I want you to know her right from the start, I want it to feel natural and

KATRINA. It does.

GAIL. And she's amazing, she is, she's so full of passion and I know

I know

why you're worried but I've been single and it's no fun, not the way I did it anyway, I was lonely and now I'm not. And I'd love to share that with you without feeling like a fool, like you're just waiting for the bomb to blow, because maybe it won't.

2021

A prestigious art gallery, Fergal's solo exhibition.

KATRINA. Somesh was really impressed.

GAIL. It is impressive.

KATRINA. Says he's going to be big.

MADDY. He already is, according to him. Not low on confidence.

GAIL. Just to get an exhibition here must be hard.

MADDY. Youngest artist to be given a solo show, he's told me what a prodigy he is.

GAIL. Good he believes in himself.

MADDY. Little bit of humility never hurt anyone.

KATRINA. Som wants to commission a series for his new restaurant.

MADDY. He'll have to get in line.

KATRINA. He wanted one of these but they're all gone.

Thought the man himself'd be here.

MADDY. No.

GAIL. Even just to lap up the praise.

MADDY. He's done that plenty, I'm sure.

KATRINA. Did you tell him when we were coming?

MADDY. I suspect that's why he's not here.

KATRINA. Too cool for his aunts now?

MADDY. We're not talking.

I mean we talk enough for him to tell me how important he's going to be, but not properly.

GAIL. There's a quote from Damien Hirst here.

MADDY. He was one of his mentors.

GAIL. Bloody hell.

He must be raking it in Mads. Not to be crude, but I mean, he must've been able to pay off his student debt, let's put it that way.

MADDY. I wouldn't know.

GAIL. Oh come on. How much are these going for?

KATRINA. The gallery takes a big cut.

GAIL. Even so.

KATRINA. Yeah, he must've made a fair amount.

MADDY. I wouldn't know.

GAIL. Is he going to help you out?

    Pause.

KATRINA. Has Mum been yet?

MADDY. She's still in France.

KATRINA. She has to see this.

MADDY. They're coming next week.

KATRINA. Wonder what Henri will think.

MADDY. Who cares.

GAIL. Dad would've loved it.

Pause.

He always wanted you to do more with your art.

MADDY. Sorry to disappoint, yet again.

GAIL. Why're you being so

Aren't you just a little bit proud?

MADDY. Of course I am.

KATRINA. If this was Walter I wouldn't be able to contain myself, every single person in this room right now would know I was his mum and this was my boy's work.

MADDY. I am proud.

KATRINA. I mean he could be the next

Take your pick, he could

Pause.

We can go, if you don't want to be here.

MADDY. He's angry at me.

KATRINA. What for?

MADDY. He thinks I should've left Rory.

Thinks I'm weak.

GAIL. What does he know, he's twenty-two.

MADDY. Everything.

He thinks it was irresponsible of me to stay.

KATRINA. You're not weak.

MADDY. Irresponsible? I'm irresponsible.

Pause.

Am I irresponsible?

KATRINA. You've stuck by him. You take your marriage vows seriously. That's not irresponsible.

Pause.

MADDY. He could pay off our debts, he could, the money he's making, it's

But he won't pay a thing unless I leave his father.

GAIL. He said that?

MADDY. And I don't blame him.

GAIL. That's not fair.

MADDY. Isn't it?

Silence.

Rory's all I've ever known, I never played the field, I never really did anything that didn't just come my way.

GAIL. That's not true.

KATRINA. Fergal has no right to dictate to you, to

MADDY. No and he's cocky and he thinks he knows it all but

If I'm lucky I've got thirty-plus years left, my boys are grown, what am I proving, what am I really proving by seeing it through?

Silence.

2022

KATRINA *and* MADDY *listen.*

GAIL. We went to this place the other side of the island, Paola
loves watersports, so we did basically everything going and
I definitely got the bug, you just feel so healthy out there,
I think that's the thing, you're spending all your time outside,
on the water, doing physical activity, in these gorgeous
surroundings, I mean you're on the edge of the world, feels
like it anyway, feels like this is how we're supposed to be.
But the best place by far, for me, was this little place called
Clearwater, we stayed at this B&B in Wells Gray Provincial
Park, in the park itself, it was run by this couple from Spain,
weirdly, they'd only been there a couple of years, they'd run
an exotic fish shop back home, family business, but in the
end they made the leap, thought it was time for something
new, which I've got such admiration for, and they'd found
themselves this beautiful patch of earth, which we pretty
much had to ourselves, and this is where we saw our first
bears, a mum and her two cubs, it was amazing, we were in
our car and they were probably where that window is, so we
watched them and God, I wasn't prepared for how special
that is. These wild creatures, just going about their business.
One thing that surprised me was how varied it is, so we were
doing watersports one day, then we were in an actual
blizzard and on a glacier when we were on the Icefields
Parkway and then a week later we were in blazing sunshine
and surrounded by vineyards in the Okanagan area, I never
worked out how to say that, Paola found it hilarious, Ock-an-
ARE-gen, Ock-AN-igan, I don't know, but that felt
completely different again.

KATRINA. So you enjoyed it?

GAIL. Oh God it was amazing.

2023

KATRINA. No, I think that's offensive.

GAIL. Why?

KATRINA. Because it suggests you think I only do things to please my husband, rather than the truth, which is I did it for myself, how it makes me feel.

GAIL. So Somesh had no opinion on the matter whatsoever?

KATRINA. You think I'd be with someone who told me I had to get work done?

GAIL. I'm sure he didn't flat-out say it's a neck lift or divorce, doesn't have to be as blunt as that.

MADDY. It looks really good.

KATRINA. Thank you, I'm pleased with it.

MADDY. How long were you in for?

KATRINA. Two and a half hours.

MADDY. That quick?

GAIL. He works in a glamorous industry though, and he likes to dress well, / he's

KATRINA. A glamorous industry? How old are you?

GAIL. What's wrong with saying a glamorous / industry?

KATRINA. Restaurants?

GAIL. Michelin-starred restaurants. And he's a good-looking man, looks after himself, I imagine he wants you to look the same.

KATRINA. You're hilarious Gail.

GAIL. Why?

KATRINA. Glamorous industry, like he's a Hollywood film producer in the thirties.

MADDY. What do they do exactly? Just pull your neck up and cut off the extra skin?

KATRINA. Pretty much.

GAIL. You didn't even have extra skin.

KATRINA. Well I did so

GAIL. You're not even fifty, is this it now, constant surgery?

KATRINA. I'd do it again, yeah.

GAIL. Do you really want to be eighty with creepily flawless skin?

KATRINA. Wouldn't mind.

MADDY. Was it expensive?

KATRINA. Not as much as I thought. It's just like getting a filling at the dentist or something.

GAIL. Not exactly.

KATRINA. No one's forcing you to do it Gail, don't worry.

MADDY. I've thought about getting something done, / but I guess

GAIL. What?

MADDY. I didn't want it looking too extreme.

KATRINA. Is mine extreme?

MADDY. No.

KATRINA. You don't have to go all Michael Jackson.

GAIL. Does everyone do this?

KATRINA. More people than you think.

GAIL. You don't need it Maddy, neither of you do.

MADDY. Just want to make the best of myself.

KATRINA. Give you confidence when you're meeting all those eligible gentlemen.

GAIL. They should want you for who you are.

KATRINA. Bloody hell, it's not changing who you are, just cutting off a bit of excess skin. You might want to think about it, standing next to Paola the whole time doesn't do you any favours.

GAIL. Charming.

MADDY. I try not to stand next to her too much, with her perfect skin.

GAIL. I don't care if I look older, I am older.

KATRINA. No doubt of that.

GAIL. Yeah yeah I've heard all the age jokes.

KATRINA. It's great you're so confident. I mean, she's a good-looking woman, looks after herself, I imagine she wants you to look the same.

GAIL. Alright alright.

KATRINA. And she works in such a glamorous industry.

GAIL. Point made.

KATRINA. Don't tell me you haven't been watching what you eat since you've been with her.

GAIL. Okay, okay, but eating healthily and having surgery are different categories, just for the record, they're not the same.

KATRINA. I'll note it in the record.

2024

Outside a church.

KATRINA. I hate when people do that though, it feels like a betrayal.

MADDY. If it helps him then

KATRINA. But she wasn't religious.

MADDY. She might've been.

KATRINA. Not properly.

MADDY. It's not like we saw her much.

KATRINA. Enough to know she wouldn't have wanted that.

GAIL. She was quite spiritual though, wasn't she?

KATRINA. What, 'cause she went to India a few times?

MADDY. They had a church wedding, remember their
wedding?

KATRINA. Yeah, 'cause he's religious, which is why he
wanted this.

GAIL. Does it matter?

KATRINA. It misrepresents who she was.

GAIL. Not really.

KATRINA. So if Som decided to have a big Muslim funeral for
me, you wouldn't mind, you wouldn't think that was a
betrayal of who I was?

GAIL. He's not religious, so that'd be strange.

KATRINA. But say he did.

GAIL. I guess I wouldn't like it.

KATRINA. And why not?

MADDY. Louise was brought up Christian at least.

KATRINA. In the same way we were, as in, not really.

MADDY. I think they do them well, the big events. I'd want
a church funeral.

KATRINA. Even though you never go to church?

MADDY. I do go.

KATRINA. When?

MADDY. Sundays.

KATRINA. Every Sunday?

MADDY. Recently, yeah.

KATRINA. Since when?

GAIL. Where?

MADDY. The last year or so. St Anne's.

GAIL. The one on the green?

MADDY *nods*.

KATRINA. Why didn't you tell us?

MADDY. Never asked.

KATRINA. Course I never asked, why would I ask, oh Maddy, have you suddenly found God?

GAIL. Wait, is that where you met Chris?

MADDY *nods*.

That makes sense now.

KATRINA. You said a mutual friend introduced you. Please say you didn't mean God.

MADDY. Well in a way

KATRINA. Oh God

MADDY. It was a mutual friend at church Katrina, don't be so

KATRINA. So are you devout now or

MADDY. I wouldn't say devout.

KATRINA. You're married to an Irish Catholic for over twenty-five years and you never go to church, you divorce and all of a sudden you're a believer?

MADDY. Well it did feel like being reborn. I guess it is kind of funny.

KATRINA. That's one word.

GAIL. I knew Chris was religious, he was very keen to let me know he was totally for gays in the church, like I should be impressed or grateful or something.

KATRINA. So I'm standing here saying Louise wasn't religious she wouldn't have wanted this but what the hell do I know, I don't even know my own sister's religious, I mean, that's something you should tell people.

MADDY. You hadn't even noticed, I haven't changed.

KATRINA. I'd say it's a change.

MADDY. It's just something I'm doing for me.

GAIL. Even if it was just a way to meet men, it worked so

KATRINA. Why didn't you tell us?

MADDY. It's a personal thing, it's

KATRINA. You should've told us. I mean Jesus, God, am I allowed to say any of that or does it offend you now?

MADDY. You can say whatever you want.

KATRINA. You should've said.

MADDY. It's really not a / big

KATRINA. It is a big deal Maddy.

GAIL. Okay, now's not the time, we should be talking about Louise, we should be remembering her, not

KATRINA. I don't know my own sister, what can I possibly say about Louise?

2025

GAIL *and Paola's home.*

KATRINA. Surprisingly sneaky.

GAIL. It's the only way I could get you guys to talk.

Silence.

So do you think we can have a conversation, because this is really stupid, and it's gone way too far.

It's affecting the whole family. Every time I speak to Mum, all she talks about is how she's failed, to have two daughters fall out over something as small as going to church.

KATRINA. It's not about going to church.

GAIL. Alright, what is it about?

KATRINA. I've explained it plenty of times.

GAIL. Okay. Let's talk about it one last time, right now, and then we can put it behind us. Can we do that?

MADDY. I'd love that.

GAIL. Obviously we were all feeling pretty emotional, it was Louise's funeral, and I think the whole thing got blown out of proportion.

KATRINA. Totally neutral mediator then.

GAIL. I am, okay, sorry, that didn't sound neutral, I know it was important to you Katrina. Can you just tell us again what upset you so much?

KATRINA. What upset me is Maddy not telling me something really major about her life.

It wasn't the religion thing, / I mean I do have

GAIL. Okay, before you get into that, that was really clear

KATRINA. You're loving this control aren't you.

GAIL. I'm just trying to keep things clear. So, Maddy, do you want to say anything?

MADDY. I think you overreacted. I think it was ridiculous, if I'm honest. And the way you've been the past year is ridiculous too.

GAIL. Could you use / another word

KATRINA. You think it's ridiculous I want to know my own sister? God, I'm sorry, what an awful person I must be, to want to know you.

MADDY. Want to know me? You haven't spoken to me in a year!

GAIL. Let's try not to use words like / ridiculous

MADDY. I'd been going to church once a week and it hadn't come up so you guys didn't know, but when you did ask, remember, I told you, I wasn't trying to hide anything but you acted like I'd had a child or got married or I don't know left the country and neglected to tell you.

KATRINA. Finding God's bigger than all those things, it completely / changes

MADDY. Finding God? I wasn't struck down on the road to Damascus, / I was simply exploring

KATRINA. Finding God, believing in God, same thing.

MADDY. I was just taking stock, after Rory, I was just seeing if it was a fit for me, why's everything always have to be so dramatic? I'm sick of it.

KATRINA. Finding God, believing in God, it's a massive thing, sorry but it is, it affects a person's whole way of living, the way they look at other people, / the way

MADDY. For the good, surely.

KATRINA. For the good, for the bad, doesn't matter, the point is it changes your outlook and that's the kind of thing you should share with the people you say you love.

MADDY. I do love you, you know that.

KATRINA. How am I supposed to know that, you haven't spoken to me in the past year!

MADDY. You haven't spoken to me!

I've texted, written cards, I sent Walter birthday and Christmas presents, I've tried.

KATRINA. You've gone through the motions, yeah.

MADDY. Gone through the

What else was I meant to have done? What did you do?

KATRINA. You did all the things you should be seen to be doing.

MADDY. There's no pleasing you Katrina, it's never enough, you always want want want, you can never just appreciate when someone's reaching out, when someone's making the effort, if it's not the exact thing you wanted then forget it.

Pause.

GAIL. You love each other. That's a good thing, right?

Silence.

MADDY. You want a lot from people Katrina.

I give you as much as I can.

Pause.

GAIL. So, I've got the ingredients for fondue.

Pause.

It was Paola's idea. She thought it'd be a nice symbol.

KATRINA. Cheese?

MADDY. Sharing.

GAIL. Sharing a meal.

MADDY. Quite literal.

KATRINA. Quite cheesy.

MADDY. You didn't just say that.

GAIL. This whole thing was her idea actually.

She thinks most things can be solved with fondue.

KATRINA. Except a lactose intolerance, presumably.

GAIL. Yeah, I mean, probably not that, but everything else.

And she's right about most things.

2026

KATRINA. I know you'll say I'm biased, but he's really good.

GAIL. I've heard him, I know he is, but can they really manage the whole evening?

KATRINA. They're sixteen, of course they can.

GAIL. I mean their repertoire. Have they got enough for three hours of music?

KATRINA. Three hours?

GAIL. Well if we hired a band, what would they play for?

KATRINA. Two hours max, surely. With a break in between.

GAIL. Okay, two hours, it's still a long time.

KATRINA. I think Mum would love it, and isn't that the point?

MADDY. Doesn't he play more

Contemporary stuff?

KATRINA. He could learn some of Mum's music. How sweet would that be? Having your grandson playing your favourite songs for you, I think this will make the party.

MADDY. Okay. So he is willing to learn new songs? And by new I mean old.

KATRINA. Of course he is.

MADDY. Have you asked him? Because Walter has quite strong ideas when it comes to music and if, for example, he didn't happen to like Mum's favourite songs

KATRINA. He'd do it for her.

You're right, he probably wouldn't do it for anyone else, but for Nanny

MADDY. And his bandmates? Who, let's be frank, don't care about Walter's nanny.

KATRINA. We'll be paying them, they'll get over it.

GAIL. What?

KATRINA. You didn't think we'd pay them?

GAIL. I thought the whole point was to save

MADDY. I thought Walter would be doing it as a special eightieth birthday present.

KATRINA. We can't expect his mates to play for nothing, that's not fair.

GAIL. Well if we're paying them I don't know why we aren't just getting professionals.

KATRINA. Because this is more personal.

And they're just as good as some cover band, they've got talent these boys, and / enthusiasm.

MADDY. It wasn't going to be a cover band, I found a really good jazz group.

KATRINA. Mum's never expressed an interest in jazz.

MADDY. But she loves the rock Walter plays.

Pause.

Okay, you're right, it'll be special to have him play.

GAIL. We could have a proper band and have Walter play one song, like the main event.

KATRINA. Proper?

MADDY. Then we're paying twice.

GAIL. We wouldn't have to pay if they were only / playing one.

KATRINA. If it's the money, I'll pay them myself.

GAIL. No.

MADDY. No, you're right, Mum will love it.

GAIL. Just as long as he learns some of her songs. Anything from the sixties.

MADDY. Well no, not anything, I think you should be quite specific with him or we'll get two hours of The Rolling Stones.

KATRINA. Mum wouldn't mind that.

MADDY. Still, I'll make a list.

GAIL. It'll be a lovely surprise, she'll love it.

2027

Maternity ward.

KATRINA. She's absolutely gorgeous though.

MADDY. Of course she is, I think he's just a bit apprehensive about having a girl.

KATRINA. He'd be apprehensive either way, no one has any idea what they're doing.

MADDY. That's what I said, he'll work it out. He was convinced it was a boy, so I think it threw him, but they'll work it out.

KATRINA. And Zara's lovely.

MADDY. I don't think they'd given girls' names much thought, they were set on Zachary, so she became Zara.

KATRINA. I love it. And what's she going to call you?

MADDY. Nothing for a bit I wouldn't have thought. Sophie's mum wants to be called Grandma, so probably not that, but I don't know, I'll see what feels right.

KATRINA. You're a grandma!

GAIL. Has Mum been?

KATRINA. She said she'd come when they're home, you know how she is in hospitals.

GAIL. She'll love her.

MADDY. I don't know, I think she liked having grandsons after us three.

GAIL. Well she might have a granddaughter yet.

KATRINA. Great-granddaughter.

GAIL. No, I mean, she might have a granddaughter.

KATRINA. How?

MADDY. You're not

GAIL. Not me, no.

MADDY. Paola's

KATRINA. Paola's having a baby?

GAIL. We're having a baby, yeah.

KATRINA. Sorry, I didn't even know you were

MADDY. She's pregnant?

GAIL. Yeah.

MADDY. What?

GAIL. She's always wanted children and it's now or never so

   We didn't tell anyone in case it didn't work but it has and she's twelve weeks pregnant and I realise it's a shock, for a lot of reasons, and I didn't mean to, you know, steal the spotlight when it's about Connor and Sophie but being here makes it feel very real, and

KATRINA *hugs* GAIL.

   Thank you.

   Pause.

MADDY. Congratulations.

   She hugs GAIL.

GAIL. I didn't mean to make it about me, I'm sorry.

MADDY. No, it's big news.

GAIL. Massive, I still haven't got my head round it.

KATRINA. That's why you get nine months.

MADDY. Becoming a mother at fifty-five, it's

GAIL. Pretty *Daily Mail*, I know, but

   No one would raise an eyebrow if I were a man.

KATRINA. And fifty-five's the new forty so

MADDY. Fifty-six by the time it arrives.

KATRINA. Alright, forty-one, that's nothing.

GAIL. I know it's a shock.

MADDY. You've never talked about wanting kids.

GAIL. That's not true.

MADDY. Well I didn't know it was something you still

GAIL. I did want them, it just never happened so I've never talked about it because what's the point. And if I wasn't with Paola, it wouldn't be happening, but as with everything to do with Paola, she's given me the chance to do something I never thought I would.

   It feels right. Not too soon, not too late, / but

MADDY. Certainly not too soon!

GAIL. Just right.

Pause.

MADDY. I want another cuddle with Zara before they throw us out.

Thanks for coming, Connor appreciates it.

I'm happy for you.

MADDY *hugs* GAIL *again, and exits.*

Pause.

GAIL. I shouldn't have said it here, she's annoyed.

KATRINA. She'll get over it.

GAIL. I know it's a shock.

KATRINA. A brilliant surprise.

Pause.

GAIL. I'm terrified.

2028

They take their seats on a train.

GAIL. This is the bit I hate. Getting home, it always takes forever.

KATRINA. It was worth it though.

MADDY. I think Chris'd like it, maybe I'll take him for his birthday.

GAIL. You'd see it again?

MADDY. He's impossible to buy for so

KATRINA. I'd go tomorrow if I could, it was brilliant.

GAIL. I struggled to keep my eyes open, but

KATRINA. 'Cause you've had no sleep for six months.

GAIL. True.

KATRINA. I'm glad you could come though.

GAIL. I'd join you for just about anything while Paola's mum's staying.

KATRINA. Anything?

GAIL. Anything. In fact I hope it does take forever to get home. Precious extra moments of peace.

MADDY. She can't be that bad.

GAIL *looks at her.*

GAIL. And there's no end date, she refuses to set an end date.

MADDY. She must have something to get home for.

GAIL *looks at her.*

KATRINA *shakes her head.*

MADDY *smiles.*

KATRINA. What?

MADDY. All these years, I knew there had to be something wrong with Paola. And now we know.

GAIL. Her mother.

MADDY. Must be why she never wanted to go home.

KATRINA. And there's Gail thinking she couldn't bear to be apart from her.

GAIL *rests her head against the window and closes her eyes.*

MADDY. Do you think that's what Valeria used to say about us?

KATRINA. Who knows what that mad bitch used to say.

GAIL (*eyes still shut*). She wasn't a bitch.

KATRINA (*mouths to* MADDY). She was.

They smile.

(*Sings a song from the show they've just seen*.) All the depths
I wandered, every chance I squandered,
All the friends I cheated, the devils I greeted

MADDY. Shh.

KATRINA (*sings, just as loudly*). All the grief and heartache,
every stupid mistake

MADDY. Katrina.

KATRINA (*belts out*). You're still here, you're still here,
And there's nothing to fear,
While you're still here.

MADDY. People will think you're drunk.

KATRINA. Drunk on life!

MADDY. That's what a drunk person would say.

KATRINA. I don't care.

MADDY. Please.

KATRINA. You're so funny Maddy, what are you worried about?

MADDY. Annoying other people.

KATRINA. I'm just singing.

MADDY. I'm serious, please, I hate it when people are loud
on trains.

KATRINA. Okay, I'll sing quietly.

MADDY. Just don't sing at all.

KATRINA. I've got a good voice, haven't I?

MADDY. Please Katrina.

KATRINA. Okay.

I'll just hum.

She hums the tune.

MADDY. I thought he was an idiot.

KATRINA. Who? Jonny?

MADDY. For sticking around, she was horrible to him.

KATRINA. Yeah, but that's what the whole thing was

> It was about their deep connection and inexpressible, except the whole musical was trying to express it I suppose, but the bond between them.

MADDY. Yeah, well, I thought he should've left her to it a long time ago.

2029

KATRINA *is cooking*.

MADDY. So you're finding things to do?

KATRINA. Are you kidding? There are so many things, there's still not enough time.

MADDY. So you don't regret it?

KATRINA. Why on earth would I regret it?

> MADDY *shrugs*.

> I'd been planning for it for years. We wanted to retire at the same time.

MADDY. You always enjoyed your job.

KATRINA. It was alright as jobs go, but I'd been doing it a long time, it / was

GAIL. I'm so jealous.

KATRINA. Look maybe the novelty will wear off and I'll be bored in a few months, but, so this morning, I went to the market, bought these ingredients, prepared them, took my time, read up on what to drink with it, it was just a nice way to spend my time, and now Walter's doing his own thing and doesn't really need me

MADDY. He'll be back.

KATRINA. Yeah, maybe, but for now he wants nothing to do with me so I'm free to

Do whatever.

MADDY. And what's Som doing? Did he go to the market? Help carry your bags?

KATRINA. No.

GAIL. I never thought he'd retire.

KATRINA. But it's nice to spend some time with your wife now and again, novel idea I know but

MADDY. So he's enjoying it?

KATRINA. He's adjusting.

MADDY. He's finally worked out you're really annoying.

GAIL. Took him longer than I thought, smart guy like that.

KATRINA. Am I that hard to live with?

GAIL. No comment.

KATRINA. Must be.

Pause.

GAIL. There's no way I can retire in the next ten years.

MADDY. Well you did have a baby at fifty-six so what do you expect?

GAIL. Alright, I'm not complaining. But obviously, because of certain decisions I made, which make me very happy and which I don't regret one bit, I probably won't be retiring before I'm eighty.

MADDY. Not that bad.

GAIL. Not far off, at this rate.

MADDY. And you didn't even have a husband who gambled away your life savings.

Pause.

Paola will go back to work soon won't she?

GAIL. Yeah, but then there's childcare and, it's all expensive, as you know.

KATRINA. I know I'm lucky.

MADDY. The baby's retired first.

GAIL. You deserve it, you've worked hard.

KATRINA. I know I'm lucky though, most people work hard.

MADDY. Yeah, they do.

Pause.

KATRINA. Who knows, maybe this will just end up as a long holiday and I'll go back to work in a few months.

MADDY. Would they have you?

KATRINA. I didn't ask but I'd hope so.

Think they'd be surprised but

No, look, I don't want to go back, I want to enjoy this, it'd just be nice if Som did too, instead of acting like he's being punished, like he didn't choose this, we chose this together.

MADDY. Remember how Dad was when he retired.

KATRINA. He was made redundant, it's different.

MADDY. They nearly got a divorce.

KATRINA. Did they?

MADDY *nods.*

MADDY. Chris's dad died a year after retiring.

KATRINA. Great Mads, great pep talk.

MADDY. No, because your attitude's different. He says he just gave up, like that was it, he was old now and there was no point going on, so I don't think I'll ever get Chris to retire.

KATRINA. Maybe I didn't think it through.

GAIL. You did.

KATRINA. But I've done it now and

GAIL. And look at the meal you've made.

KATRINA. Thought you were going to say mess then.

GAIL. No, it smells amazing. And you never would've had time to do this before.

KATRINA. Som's not even here to enjoy it.

GAIL. We are.

KATRINA. No, I know, thank you.

GAIL. How've you managed to get us feeling sorry for you being retired?

KATRINA. I didn't mean to

GAIL. Just think, you can get off your face tonight and spend the whole day tomorrow recovering and not even have to ring in and pretend you're genuinely sick.

KATRINA. That's true.

MADDY. Did you ever actually do that?

KATRINA. Are you kidding?

MADDY. I never have.

KATRINA. Oh, you haven't lived.

Fake sick days are like a whole other kind of day.

GAIL. Magical.

KATRINA. They are, they're magical.

MADDY. I'd feel too guilty, there'd be no point.

KATRINA. No no no, I insist you do it once, Mads, while you still can. It's amazing. You know you're supposed to be at work so it feels like stolen time

MADDY. It is.

KATRINA. No, it's this time you'd written off, you never thought you'd see it again, but suddenly you're reunited, and it's like, imagine you had an old friend, let's call her Mary-Lou

GAIL. Mary-Lou?

KATRINA. And you thought Mary-Lou had died, but one day she just knocks on your door, imagine how you'd feel.

MADDY. I'd want to know who misreported her death.

KATRINA. You'd feel, all that time, all that time I could've spent with you if only I'd known, and so you embrace her tighter, you hold her closer than you ever would have, because maybe actually she wasn't even one of your favourite people, but because she's been gone and now she's suddenly in front of you, you're overcome with gratitude and emotion and nostalgia and fondness, and somehow, even though, as I say, there may be other people you love far more, somehow this is the most precious time you'll ever have.

Where's the wine I researched for two hours?

GAIL *finds the wine.*

Right, we're getting wasted Maddy, and tomorrow, tomorrow morning you're going to call work and say you're sick and you're going to see what I'm talking about.

2030

The top of Ben Nevis, at night. The stars are out.

MADDY. Thanks for doing this with me.

GAIL. Nearly killed me but don't worry about it.

MADDY. I knew you could do it.

GAIL. I didn't.

KATRINA. Worth it though.

GAIL. I'll give you that.

MADDY. Stunning.

They stare up at the sky.

Chris was jealous, wanted to come, but I said it's just the three of us.

KATRINA. Mum was annoyed you didn't choose something more accessible.

MADDY. I told her we'd do a tea somewhere, she was fine.

Never been one for climbing mountains.

GAIL. Don't blame her.

KATRINA. You know when we went camping for your fortieth.

MADDY. Yeah.

GAIL. I know what you're going to say.

KATRINA. Mum

GAIL. About the camping?

KATRINA. Yeah, so Mum and Dad didn't camp.

MADDY. What?

KATRINA. They stayed at a local B&B.

MADDY. But they had a tent.

GAIL. Just a decoy.

MADDY. What?

KATRINA. They didn't want to offend you since it was your birthday and they knew things weren't easy so they pretended to camp, put up the tent, unrolled the sleeping bags, / and just

GAIL. Which they had no intention of sleeping in.

KATRINA. And they just drove to a B&B, made sure they were back at the campsite early in the morning.

MADDY. The cheeky

KATRINA. And I'd just had Walter, so I was camping, oh and Eric had left, so I was literally in a tent on my own with a baby but Mum and Dad, don't worry about them, they were living it up at a B&B.

MADDY. What if I'd gone to the tent to borrow something or one of the boys had needed something or

GAIL. You know what Dad was like with his sleep.

MADDY. They could've just said.

GAIL. They didn't want to offend you.

MADDY. Was I that easily offended?

GAIL. You'd organised everything and

MADDY. Wasn't the best trip.

GAIL. No.

MADDY. You had a bee in your bonnet about champagne, how we absolutely had to have champagne.

GAIL. Which leads me nicely to

She digs in her bag.

MADDY. You didn't bring champagne?

KATRINA. Oh, amazing.

GAIL *is empty-handed.*

GAIL. No, but how good would that've been?

KATRINA. Why'd you do that, I really want a glass of champagne now.

MADDY. That would've been cool.

GAIL. Yeah, I should've thought of it, sorry.

Just didn't want to make my bag any heavier.

Pause.

MADDY. I got Zara some of those glow-in-the-dark stars for her ceiling, like Fergal had.

KATRINA. Didn't I get him those?

MADDY. And I remembered how Rory had arranged them on the ceiling so they were in the same position as the real stars, if Fergal had been looking up at the night sky from his bed.

Pause.

Wasn't all bad.